AN AMERICAN FAMILY

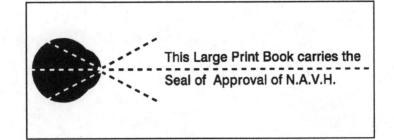

This Large Print Book carries the
Seal of Approval of N.A.V.H.

AN AMERICAN FAMILY

A MEMOIR OF HOPE AND SACRIFICE

KHIZR KHAN

THORNDIKE PRESS
A part of Gale, a Cengage Company

GALE
A Cengage Company

Farmington Hills, Mich • San Francisco • New York • Waterville, Maine
Meriden, Conn • Mason, Ohio • Chicago

Copyright © 2017 by Khizr Khan.
Photos courtesy of the Khan Family.
Thorndike Press, a part of Gale, Cengage Learning.

ALL RIGHTS RESERVED
Thorndike Press® Large Print Popular and Narrative Nonfiction.
The text of this Large Print edition is unabridged.
Other aspects of the book may vary from the original edition.
Set in 16 pt. Plantin.

**LIBRARY OF CONGRESS CIP DATA ON FILE.
CATALOGUING IN PUBLICATION FOR THIS BOOK
IS AVAILABLE FROM THE LIBRARY OF CONGRESS.**

ISBN-13: 978-1-4328-4557-5 (hardcover)
ISBN-10: 1-4328-4557-8 (hardcover)

Published in 2017 by arrangement with Random House, an imprint and division of Penguin Random House LLC

Printed in Mexico
1 2 3 4 5 6 7 21 20 19 18 17

To Ghazala,
our children,
and our grandchildren

CONTENTS

INTRODUCTION

When I was a young boy in Pakistan, my grandfather used to tell me stories in the moonlight before I fell asleep. Some nights he would read to me Iqbal or Rumi or another Persian poet, and some nights he would sketch out a parable, adapting a snippet of classical literature or a lesson from the Qur'an so that a child might understand. He was a wise and kind man, soft-spoken and thoughtful, who believed in two things above all else: education and the fundamental dignity of each person. Many of his stories, indeed most of them, were variations on those themes, lessons of integrity, mercy, and charity.

One sweltering summer night when I was eight or nine years old, he sat on the edge of my cot and paraphrased some Rumi: "So what if you are thirsty? Always be a river for everyone."

That idea lingered with me. When I was

grown and married and had children of my own, I often repeated those sentences to them. The translation from Persian to English is not technically precise, but the sentiment is unambiguous. Always try to comfort others, even if you are suffering. Offer compassion to your neighbor, to the stranger, to the roiling, boisterous masses of humanity. Share your gifts with the world, no matter how meager those gifts may be.

Those twelve words, I've learned in my sixty-seven years, are a good and useful guide to a life well lived.

I have known thirst, as we all have, though it has not defined my life by any means. I was raised by parents and grandparents who never had much but always enough, and who loved me deeply. I have been married to an angelic woman for forty-two years, and together we raised three happy, healthy boys who each grew up to prosper in his own way. Though I came from a poor family, I was able to be educated at some of the finest universities in the world. I became a successful attorney. Many of those blessings and many others were made possible because my wife, Ghazala, and I immigrated to the United States, and had the chance to avail ourselves of its boundless promises of equality and freedom.

10

Still, there have been times of thirst. I grew up in an autocratic society, where the freedoms I cherish in America did not exist. There were years, when I was much younger, when I had barely enough rupees in my pocket to feed myself, and there were nights when I had no proper place to lay my head. But in the long context of my life, those were minor inconveniences, momentary troubles.

Then there was this: In 2004, our middle son, Humayun, was killed. Humayun was a captain in the United States Army, and he was killed by a suicide bomber outside Baghdad. The Army posthumously awarded him a Bronze Star and a Purple Heart, and he was buried in Arlington National Cemetery with full military honors. Because he died early in the war, and because he was one of the first Muslim American soldiers to sacrifice his life in Iraq, reporters were interested in Humayun. I spoke to a few of them, mostly after his burial, and the stories they wrote were respectful and accurate.

Then the world moved on, as it should. Ghazala and our sons and I grieved in private, slowly rebuilding our shattered lives. In Rumi's construction, we were desiccated by thirst. It was difficult to breathe at times, let alone be a river.

A dozen years passed. We remained, through all of them, private people, which is our nature. We were just another middle-class family in a small Virginia city, living our anonymous lives.

In the summer of 2016, however, we were invited to speak at the Democratic National Convention. We were hesitant, but Hillary Clinton, the candidate we favored, had planned a tribute to Humayun that night. She'd spoken eloquently — and apolitically — about his sacrifice in the past. It seemed only proper that we stand for him, too. So we took the podium, as I put it that night, "as patriotic American Muslims with undivided loyalty to our country." Ghazala was too overcome with emotion to speak, but I addressed the Republican candidate, Donald Trump, directly. Over a period of many months, he had repeatedly called for Muslims to be banned from entering the country. I reminded him that if his position had been policy, our son never would have become an American. I reminded him, too, that he had disrespected women, judges, minorities, even the leadership of his own party — a mean and persistent sorting of people into those who would be welcome in Trump's America and those who would not. His was a campaign fundamentally at odds with American values, with the founding principles of a great and inclusive nation.

"Let me ask you," I said. "Have you even read the United States Constitution?" I held up a pocket-sized version. "I will gladly lend you my copy."

I had carried that Constitution with me for years. It was dog-eared and creased, marked with notations and highlights. I had studied it, and I had long cherished the words, the ideas, embodied within. To celebrate it publicly, to hold it up as a reminder of what America is supposed to be, seemed the most patriotic thing I could do.

Having said our piece, we expected, perhaps naïvely, to return to our quiet lives.

That did not happen. Since that night, I have been asked to speak at many more gatherings, large and small. My remarks always focus on the same key ideas: extolling the Constitution and the rule of law, celebrating equal protection and equal dignity for all Americans, professing the need to stand up to words and deeds that violate the ideals patriots hold dear.

I am always grateful for the opportunity

to share my thoughts, and humbled that others want to hear what I have to say. I am heartened that such audiences, enthusiastic and passionate, are out there, and in such great numbers. At the same time, it is never easy. As a family, we still prefer our privacy.

I have frequently been asked questions that are too complicated to answer in brief. Most common among them are inquiries about how we came to this place — about how, after sixty-seven years on this earth, the son of Pakistani farmers came to be an outspoken advocate for America, for the Constitution, for the great blessings of freedom and liberty bestowed upon us by heroic men and women more than two hundred years ago. I always feel compelled to answer, because this country has given us so much, but there is never time to do the whole truth justice. So this is my attempt to explain more fully. It is, by design, my story. It is in part Ghazala's, too, and our family's, but I have tried to respect the privacy of our two sons, of their wives, their children, and my many siblings, as much as possible.

Parts of it have been extremely difficult to put to paper, as I suppose it would be for anyone who is by nature solitary, who prefers to keep his own counsel rather than burden others with his troubles. Some moments I've never shared with anyone, including Ghazala, whom I love beyond measure, beyond words: I never kept secrets from her, but there have been times when I have not wanted to trouble her with my temporary discomforts. But to fully explain why I love America, why I am a patriot, I have put even those moments into words.

Because so what if I am thirsty? We are all thirsty, from time to time.

I will try to be a river, to the best of my ability.

Khizr Khan, Charlottesville, July 2017

CHAPTER 1
SHOELESS IN A SHAFT OF SUNLIGHT

I carried a sheaf of papers almost as thick as my hand to the third floor of my dorm on New Campus, just across the canal from the academic buildings. My room was small and sparse, just a metal desk with a matching chair and a small electric fan to blow away a little of the Pakistani heat. It suited me. My clothes were tucked neatly into a closet, and my bed was a cotton mattress on the floor. There had been an iron bed frame, but it was too short for me, so out it went. Sleeping on the floor was better for my back, anyway.

I slipped off my shoes and dropped the pile on the desk. It landed with a flat, dull thump. There was no textbook for my course in Comparative Constitutions of the World, just this pile of unbound papers, curated by the professor and kept behind the counter at a cramped bookshop in the old Anarkali bazaar. It was the oldest marketplace in Lahore, a kaleidoscope of fruit stands and food carts and stalls that sold cloth and spices and produce and a thousand other goods, almost anything anyone might want to buy. The air was perfumed with cardamom and the smoky-sweet tang of grilled meat that gradually curdled into a stink of horse dung and diesel and human sweat; and the alleys were crowded with rickshaws and taxis overflowing with passengers and packages. Horses pulled buggies and left droppings on the paths. Skinny men hauled large carts with unreasonably heavy loads. In the jittering splendor of Anarkali, I always noticed them, saw what poverty could force a meek man to do to earn a few rupees.

It'd taken me forty minutes by bus to get to the shop, then another forty back through the unrelenting traffic of Lahore. When I got to my room, a shaft of late afternoon sun slanted through the window.

Printed across the top page was CONSTITUTION OF THE UNITED STATES. Below that, deeper in the stack, were the constitutions of the Soviet Union, a fat ream of interminable articles and clauses, and of West Germany, slimmer, I would discover, but just as dull, as well as the Magna Carta. I hadn't bothered skimming any of them as

I rode the bus back through the potholed and rutted streets. It seemed too much trouble to be juggling pages of legalese while bouncing beside sweaty commuters. But now, standing alone at my desk with the kind of half-bored curiosity one tends to feel in a burgeoning dusk, I turned the page.

The Constitution was not on the next one. Instead, the title on the second page was DECLARATION OF INDEPENDENCE.

Those were curious words, the way they were arranged into an aggressive noun. I rolled them around in my head. To declare your independence. *I declare my independence.*

My spine tingled, straightened, a quick, involuntary spasm. I'd grasped, in that moment, a remarkable insight, a great and improbable truth I'd never conceived to be possible.

In January 1972, I was a college graduate, fluent in three languages and studying law. But I knew almost nothing of America. Very few of us at the University of the Punjab did. The little I did know I'd learned from movies with forgettable titles, and those mostly involved cowboys. I'd studied none of the history or politics. I had no concept of independence as something that could be declared or demanded. If you have lived half of your life under martial law and the rest in a swirl of political chaos, Western ideals aren't readily in your orbit. The idea that people could simply announce they were taking charge of their own affairs was so bold as to be unimaginable. It had never occurred to me.

There's a long, elegant sentence at the beginning of the Declaration of Independence about how when *people dissolve the political bands which have connected them to another,* they owe mankind the courtesy of explaining why. Even ignorant of the specifics, I recognized that sentence for what it was: a polite introduction to treason, the codification of a rebellion.

We hold these truths to be self-evident . . .

I shifted my weight from one foot to the other, too intrigued to stop reading long enough to find my chair.

. . . that all men are created equal, that they are endowed by their Creator with certain unalienable Rights, that among these are Life, Liberty and the pursuit of happiness . . .

The thing is, those truths were not remotely self-evident. Not to a young man in Pakistan and not to most people in the whole of human existence. It did not matter if men were *created* equal. From my own experiences, I knew that men were sorted into strongmen and dictators; rich men who didn't need a ration card to buy a bag of sugar; desperate, determined men who were beaten by police in the street; and, mostly, masses of the poor and illiterate who struggled to survive from season to season. Rights were not unalienable. There were only tenuous privileges granted by capricious powers, which meant that they were not rights at all. There were no rights.

I don't know how long I stood there, shoeless in that shaft of sunlight. The Declaration is not a long document, only thirteen hundred words, but I read conscientiously, deliberately, too enthralled to move. I'd never been so struck by a few sentences, ideas and ideals that, for a moment, removed me from where I was to where it was possible to be. Most Americans inherit the principles in those first paragraphs as a birthright. To many of them, the words are just dusty history, studied in a civics class, half-forgotten. But to me, a student in Pakistan, they were radically charged — as revolutionary as they'd been two centuries earlier when they were fixed to paper.

I kept reading, through a list of grievances. I had no idea who'd written the Declaration, nor against whom those grievances had been lodged. But then I realized: That didn't matter. This wasn't only foreign history. This was *our* story, too. The story of Pakistan, the story of the subcontinent, the story, really, of all colonized peoples everywhere and in every era. This was my story and my parents' story and my grandparents' story before them.

Except the Americans apparently had figured out a different ending than we had.

I shook off a creeping numbness in my legs, pulled the Declaration from its place atop the pile, and sat down on my mattress on the floor, my back against the wall. I'd read it first with a student's curiosity. Now I had to read it as a researcher on the cusp of a breakthrough, picking through the details, examining the clauses and phrases, fitting them into a precise and unified theory. To know the whole, I needed to understand each piece.

I was like a lonesome islander who'd found a bottle washed up on the beach, a secret script tucked inside that told of a wonderland, a fantastical place that existed, improbably and perhaps impossibly, far across the ocean. I needed to explore it, to set my mind deep into the words, let them absorb me, take me to a place so different from where I was.

"Okay, we have to go, Muazzam."

My father smiled at me. Like everyone else, he called me by my middle name. He looked at his watch, a Camy on a gold band that wrapped around his wrist, but we all knew it was getting late in the day. The sky above my grandparents' courtyard blushed with the first pinks of sunset. "The bus will come soon," he said. "Time to pack up."

In the morning, my grandfather had walked to the butcher to buy meat in his neighborhood in Gujranwala, a small industrial city an hour north of Lahore. Sometimes he would get a cut of goat and sometimes beef and sometimes, but not often because it was special and expensive, chicken. Sometimes, the butcher would whisper, "I won't sell you meat today," which meant the cuts in his shop were fatty or rancid or nearly so, and he would send my grandfather away with nothing. Today, my grandfather had bought goat.

My mother and my grandmother cooked in the kitchen at the back of my grandparents' courtyard. There was rice, of course, and also a sweet rice because it was sort of a celebration, all of us together for

23

the first time in a month. Vegetables were washed under water drawn from the kitchen pump. There was no refrigerator, and no electricity anyway, so what vegetables ended up on the table was a crafty calculus of what was available from the market and what would keep the longest. Turnips, potatoes, onions, and garlic could wait in a cool and dark corner until they sprouted eyes and new green shoots. Spinach would wilt in the summer heat and so had to be eaten immediately, but lettuce and cucumbers could survive a day or two.

I played with my brother and my sister on the packed clay of the courtyard. I was six years old, the first of my parents' ten children. A new sibling came on a regular two-year cycle. When I turned eight, there were four of us, three brothers and a sister; at ten, there was another brother, and so on until there were five brothers and five sisters. But then, when I was six, it was just the three of us.

We ate in the middle of the afternoon. My father waited to sit until his own father sat, and then waited some more until his mother told him to sit. He always deferred to his parents. If my grandmother had announced that the sky had turned green, he would have nodded and said, "Yes, Mother." That was how a child treated his elders, with respect even if it meant that sort of silly deference.

Over dinner, the adults spoke mainly of the extended family, of who was marrying whom, where a cousin had moved and why, about a nephew who'd finished university and begun a professional career. The afternoon wore on until the bright azure above the courtyard dulled to dusty cobalt edged with pink and orange. My father looked at his watch and told us it was time to leave.

I had come to hate sunsets. Sunsets meant saying goodbye.

My mother fussed with my brother and sister, found their shoes, settled them. The rest of us sorted the leftover food, then stacked the plates in the center of a small tablecloth that we bound up by the corners and tied into a satchel I always insisted on carrying. Then the five of us went through the door from the courtyard to the street.

The bus stop was about a quarter of a mile away, and we walked along the side of the brick road. Dread settled into my stomach, and with every step it rose, burbling up through my chest, into my throat. I hated those walks.

The bus came. My father got on first, which he usually did, so he could survey the seats, who was sitting where, and, if he had to, ask someone to move so he could keep his family together. People were surprisingly accommodating to such a request. My brother and sister followed. My mother hugged me. "I love you, Muazzam," she said. "We'll see you soon." She kissed me on the top of the head and climbed on the bus.

I ran to the other side, into the street. I always hoped they would sit on the street side, where passengers weren't pressed against the windows to see what the sidewalk vendors were hawking, and I could watch them for a few moments while the bus idled and coughed exhaust into the evening air. I waved and smiled an oversized smile.

The bus pulled away and I ran to the other side of the street, where there was a small hill. I scrambled to the top. The road was long and flat, and from up there I could watch the bus shrink into the distance until it was only a tiny blur. My eyes teared. I started to cry, and then I sobbed, great, hyperventilating heaves, alone at the top of a hill in the dusk.

I lived with my grandparents, as I'd done for so long that I had no memory of having been sent there. There was no particular reason, other than my grandparents were retired and had no children at home and wanted my father's firstborn to raise. I never asked why, never begged my mother to let me get on the bus, never pleaded to come home, because to do so would have been ungrateful and rude. Why shouldn't I be content with this blessing? My grandparents didn't have to divide their attention among three children. I was their only concern. Besides, one did not question his elders. But that didn't make it hurt any less.

They schooled me at home. They believed there were many varieties of children in the local schools, and they preferred I not associate with several of them — the disobedient, the slothful, the unserious. When I got a little older and learned to play cricket, they would walk with me to the pitch and wait and watch, and when it was over, when the other boys went wherever it was boys went, they walked me home.

There were two neighbor boys who came to play, but not often. And I had pets for a while, two chickens that hatched from eggs my grandparents hid in the nests pigeons had burrowed into one of the mud walls of the house. When they were little and yellow and downy, I chased them around with a handful of feed and a bowl of water. When they were grown, with talons and beaks, they chased me around, hungry or maybe playing but scaring me onto my cot until my grandmother shooed them away. But other than that, and visits from my parents, it was mostly just my grandparents and me.

I did learn, though. My grandparents were friends with some local teachers who would give them the textbooks the other children were studying. History, civics, Islamic studies, mathematics. Books were my constant companions, my reliable friends. I read during the day and at night in the courtyard by the glow of the kerosene lamp, and when it was extinguished and I was supposed to be asleep, I would find a volume I'd hidden under my pillow and read in the moonlight.

Most of my books were in Urdu, the letters like calligraphy inked from right to left across the page. But my grandfather also taught me Persian and English, the languages of the educated and the civil service. He'd been a regional supervisor with the Indian railroad, and spoke both fluently. One summer, he took to writing a single, simple word on a sheet of paper — *eat* or *go* — under which he would draw twenty-six lines. "Now," he would say, "I want you to write me twenty-six sentences with that word." The first ones were easy — *I go. You go. We go* — but then I would have to puzzle out tenses — *I have eaten. You will eat. They ate.*

By the time my grandparents enrolled me in sixth grade, I was already doing seventh-grade work. I was the new and precocious child at school, the teacher's assistant, always called on in class.

My parents and my brothers and sisters came every month, sometimes twice, for years. The women cooked, the men talked, the children played. And when sunset came and the dread began to ferment, I would walk them to the bus stop and run into the street, wave and scramble up the hill and watch the bus disappear into the distance and sit there, sobbing, until I'd cried myself dry. The sound of a child's weeping is still unbearable to me.

Then I walked back to my grandparents' house, through the door and across the courtyard to my room. I never let them see me cry. I never told them I wanted to go home. I would have hurt their feelings terribly. I pretended everything was fine, as so many of us learn to do in some way or another.

The summer heat never felt unbearable, even when the temperature rose to 110 degrees and we'd have to close the door to the street so the sun wouldn't bake the interior walls. There was no air conditioning or even fans, so my grandparents and I would move our cots into the courtyard where there was a touch of evening cool. There were a few red bricks embedded in the clay, and I would position my cot so the legs would rest on them and not sink into the ground under my weight.

I liked to watch the moon. After the kerosene lamp had been put out for the night, I'd wait for it to edge over the wall of the courtyard, fat and silver, and slowly glide to the other side. My grandfather would often come and sit at the edge of my bed and tell me a story, some bit of Rumi or Saadi he'd reread. He was a tall, slim man with a full head of white hair, partial to long walks in the early morning and the early evening, his left hand curled around a burgundy cane. He was highly educated, and believed no man is complete until his education is complete.

He told me stories at night because that was the best time to tell them, when they could linger undisturbed until morning, marinating in my dream sleep.

"Do you know how an ordinary stick becomes a ney?" he asked me one night. A ney is a type of flute, the kind that makes the saddest and sweetest music. I shook my head, unsure what he meant. He stared at me patiently for a moment before he spoke again. My grandfather had a deep baritone voice but it was preternaturally gentle; I never heard him speak a harsh word. He was the kind of man who preferred silence to unkindness.

"A stick becomes a ney," he said finally, "only after a sharp piece of metal drills many holes in it."

That was from Rumi, a parable in one sentence.

Islamic Studies was part of the standard curriculum in school, a mix of history and dogma, how to pray, when to pray. I rarely prayed. My grandparents did so regularly, but to them that was a matter of genuine faith, not an arbitrary rule to be followed because of an imam's decree. If I might someday come to pray with each muezzin's call, that was to be because I'd found it in my heart to do so, not because I was following orders. Without an underlying faith, the rituals are meaningless, little more than crowd control.

"I read an interesting story today," my grandfather told me one night, though in a way that suggested he'd read it many times before and believed I was only now ready to hear it. He sat on my bed in his white pajamas, bathed in moonlight. "It's about the great hajj," he said — the pilgrimage to Mecca that all devout and able Muslims are required to make at least once in their life.

"Many years ago, the Prophet, peace be upon him, said that he would be making his last pilgrimage," he said. "So of course, many people wanted to go with him, to be with the Prophet on his last hajj. There was one man, very devout, who prepared very carefully. Remember, back then, this was a long walk through the desert, and you had to have food and water and shelter. And this man, he gathered all of those things and portioned them out, had exactly enough for each day of the pilgrimage. And he felt very blessed because he had never made the hajj, and now he was going with the Prophet, peace be upon him, to Mecca.

"The night before they were to leave, there was a knock on his door. He opened it, and there stood a woman with two small children. 'Please,' she said, 'we have been traveling and we have no money and no food and my children have not eaten for two days. Please help us.' "

"Well, the man knew he had only enough

food and water for himself to complete the hajj."

My grandfather raised his eyebrows at me, to make sure I understood the quandary facing the pilgrim.

"What could he do? The children were starving. He gave them some food, and he gave the woman some food, and he gave them water. Then he asked how much farther they had to travel, and they told him and it was quite far so he gave them more food and water. And when he was done, he had nothing left for himself. So in the morning, when the Prophet and his followers left, he stayed behind."

He rearranged himself on the bed and let that hang for a moment, this terrible breach of religious duty.

"Days went by," he continued, "and the Prophet finally returned, and he heard about this man who did not go on the hajj. He said, 'Bring him to me, I want to see this man.' And the other people brought the man, expecting he would be chastised for abandoning his duty."

He paused again, a moment of high dramatic tension.

"The Prophet put his hand on the man's shoulder," he said. He tightened his face into a serious expression, as if he were about to make a profound announcement. "And he turned to the crowd and said, 'This man, his hajj is the first to be accepted.' The first! This man who didn't even go! The Prophet said, 'He helped a woman and children in need. He sacrificed and shared what he had. This — *this!* — is what I have been teaching you for twenty-three years.' "

I understood immediately, understood the point of the story, understood why my grandfather never forced me to pray. I fell asleep that night thinking of faith and charity, of the futility of piety without generosity of spirit. That was the essence of my Islamic studies, distilled by my grandfather under the moon on a hot summer night.

In the fall of 1961, when I was in sixth grade, the president of Pakistan came to speak to the schoolchildren. This was of course a tremendous honor, and we arrived at school that day all scrubbed and clean. In the late morning, we lined up in single file, all the boys from the middle school, gleaming in our white *shalwar kameez.* Our teachers led us outside and across the street to a park where the grass had been worn away by children playing cricket and football. Police officers and soldiers formed a cordon on the perimeter, and we threaded through a gap in their ranks. The youngest boys, including me, sat in a row in the dirt in front of a microphone on a stand; the older boys sat behind us, ordered by ascending age. The teachers stood in the back, and local politicians and functionaries and businessmen and landlords on the flanks, all of us waiting.

The president's motorcade appeared on the street behind the park, a big black sedan adorned with fluttering flags and trailed by drab brown military vehicles, all of them crawling from right to left, then turning, stopping. An aide opened the rear door of the sedan, and President Mohammed Ayub Khan stepped out, shook a few hands, and walked to the microphone.

He was magnificent in his khaki uniform, medals shining on his left breast, a blue-and-white sash slashing from his shoulder to his waist. Before he was president, Ayub Khan was one of the country's greatest military leaders, a veteran of the Burmese campaigns in World War II and the first commander of the Pakistani Army.

He had been president for almost three years, since the end of 1958, a position he'd appointed himself to by exiling the previous president in a bloodless coup that was no more or less traumatic than the rest of

Pakistan's short political history.

The British had partitioned their colonial holdings on the subcontinent in 1947, drawing borders meant roughly to separate three hundred million Hindus and sixty million Muslims into the independent nations of India and Pakistan (which was further bifurcated into West and East Pakistan). But because clans and sects don't fall neatly on one side or the other of an arbitrary and artificial line, millions migrated across the borders, internally displaced in their own new countries. With no history of self-governance, Pakistan almost immediately fell into chaos. The first prime minister, Liaquat Ali Khan, was assassinated in 1951, and there were six more prime ministers and five heads of state before Ayub Khan took control.

He was an autocrat who began what became known as Pakistan's first military period. He declared martial law, abolished political parties and arrested perceived opponents, took control of the newspapers, and, under a rule called Section 144, outlawed public gatherings of more than four people. He was also enormously popular, at least in the beginning, because life is in some ways simpler when a strongman is in charge. Some nights, I would listen as my grandfather debated his friends who were nostalgic for the colonial era. "How much easier it was then!" they would say. "You got up and went to work and came home and lived your life. No one had to worry if this one was corrupt or if that one was smart." My grandfather disagreed — an educated man will almost always see a challenging freedom as worthier than mindless obedience, he maintained — but he understood why his friends might want a simpler life.

Sitting in the dirt with my schoolmates, I was too young to understand any of that. I was awestruck: Ayub Khan was the president, and that was all that mattered. He spoke only briefly, and he said the banal things — study hard, be good citizens, follow the rules — that important people are supposed to say to schoolboys. Then he stepped toward us. We instinctively stood, and he went down the line, shaking our hands one by one. He was a tall man, and I was at eye level with his chest. His medals glinted in the late morning sun, bright and brilliant, like jewels, reflecting a long-ago bravery.

When I was thirteen years old, my grandmother came down with a terrible fever.

Days went by and it didn't break. My grandfather was frantic with worry. She was so sick that the three of us went to my parents' house so my mother could nurse her back to health.

My parents took her to a doctor, who diagnosed typhoid and gave her some medicine.

After so many years, we all were together. My parents, my brothers and sisters, my grandparents. All of us. I was happy. I was home.

Her fever lingered.

I came home from school one afternoon. My mother reached for me as I walked in the door, wrapped herself around me, held me.

After the burial, my parents asked my grandfather to stay with us permanently. But he was comfortable in his own neighborhood and his own house, even as it echoed now with loneliness. I went there not long after to collect my things. I took some of my grandmother's clothes, too. She wore a fragrance that smelled of roses, and it lingered on the fabric. I kept them in my new room, and whenever I missed her, I would hold them to my face and breathe in what remained. I kept them for years, until the scent was gone and they were just simple cloths again.

My parents were farmers. We didn't live on the farm but rather in a house in the western end of Gujranwala. It was similar to my grandparents' home, a kitchen and bed-rooms and a sitting room surrounding an open courtyard, except for a stairway up to a storeroom and a covered veranda on top of the lower rooms. Every morning, my father would walk two or three miles to the land his father had left him, which had been left to him by his father. He grew fields of wheat and sugarcane, irrigated by a small canal cut from the big Upper Chenab Canal and banked by slopes of emerald grass, and also vegetables — cucumbers, carrots, and tomatoes in the summer, mustard greens and collards in the winter — that vendors would haul away in the morning to sell in the market.

We had two cows that were milked twice a day, and one of my chores, once I'd moved to my parents' house, was to collect the milk, usually in the evening, in the magic hour, when the light was thick and golden. I'd carry it home, where half would be set aside for drinking and the rest my mother would ferment into kefir and churn into butter and work into ghee. Once or twice a month, my father would give her a few rupees and she'd buy staples in the market, lentils and rice and flour and cooking oil. My mother would tip a porter who lugged it all home for her, and then I would help her put everything away. Typically, one of her daughters would have been her kitchen helper, but my eldest sister was only nine.

My mother cooked every meal at home, all of them simple, just one main dish, instead of the assortment of sides and courses typical of more affluent families. We had meat and bread or a vegetable and rice. But there was always enough, even if it meant everyone sometimes had a little less.

My four brothers and two sisters all slept in the same room, their cots arranged like a puzzle. I was given my own, which had been a small guestroom when I lived with my grandparents. That was one of the privileges of being the eldest child, I suppose. I also never had to wear a coat or a pair of shoes an older brother had outgrown, but rather was first in line for new ones that would be passed down from me. If my mother made a new dish, the oldest son would have the privilege of tasting it first. There are small pleasures bestowed upon the firstborn.

There are, too, burdens. I was constantly aware that each privilege also carried a responsibility, that each little perk was also an investment in me. "Look at your brother, how hard he studies," my mother would tell the others. "You should be like him." I was the model the others were expected to follow, and I knew it. Everything I was given, no matter how seemingly insignificant or practically necessary, represented something one of them was not given. Each day, I accrued another tick of familial debt; I owed my parents, my brothers, my sisters . . . *something,* even if that was merely a duty not to fail.

So I studied. I walked five miles to school every day and then five miles back, a coat pulled around me in the winter, an umbrella shielding me in the rainy season, but always walking. (Yes, years later I would be that curmudgeonly stereotype telling his children how I used to walk five miles to and from school.) Some days, I would take my books up to the farm and read on the green banks of the canal or under the shade tree by the water pump. I finished all my assignments and received excellent marks, and by the time I was graduating from high school at seventeen, there was no question that I would continue to university.

College was another privilege and a profound responsibility. I was the first in my family, going back through the generations, to enroll in university. My grandfather, as wise and educated as he was, had graduated only from high school; the rest of his education came from his own reading, his own desire to learn. I was making a leap forward not only for myself, but also for my brothers and sisters, blazing a trail for them to follow. As much as I wanted to continue my studies, I never lost sight of the responsibility to succeed, for myself and my family.

The University of the Punjab, which had a campus in Gujranwala, was subsidized by the government, so the fees weren't particularly expensive, the equivalent of perhaps $10 or $15 a semester. But if you are a farmer with seven children to feed and another on the way, even that is not an insignificant sum. Still, my parents came up with the funds. And then, because the campus was seven miles away, they bought me a bicycle. It was a new one, too, and it cost them a hundred rupees, more than $20. I was so grateful. I kept that bicycle spotless; if I came to a puddle of mud in the road that I couldn't swerve around, I would get off and walk the bike, avoiding as much of the muck as possible, not letting it splatter on the spokes and the frame. I knew the money spent on the bicycle could have been spent on something else for someone else. Those were another hundred rupees invested in me. I could not let them down.

I stopped on the far side of the train tracks, which ran parallel to the Grand Trunk Road, the main boulevard running through Gujranwala and connecting all the cities in Punjab. I had to cross first the road and then the tracks to get to campus in the mornings, and the tracks and then the road to return home. There was a guard at the crossing who would lower a pole across the road and wave a red flag to stop traffic if a train was coming, but pedestrians and people on bicycles would ignore him if the locomotive was far enough away.

There was no train approaching, but I stopped anyway. The G.T. Road — that's what everyone called it — was clogged with protesters, a procession stalled by a phalanx of police. Orders to disperse came through a bullhorn, the amplified voice echoing off the low shops fronting the road.

The crowd stayed where it was.

The voice boomed again: "Baton charge!"

Dozens of police, a smear of khaki pants and dark gray shirts and white helmets, pushed up the street, swinging black clubs. The demonstrators tried to backpedal into

43

the throng. Some stumbled and fell to the pavement, where they curled up under a slashing rain of batons.

The protests had started in the fall of 1968 in Karachi and Lahore and Rawalpindi, and had spread, in the winter of 1969, to the smaller cities like Gujranwala, a dusty town of factories that stamped out kitchen utensils and ceiling fans and the like. The popularity Ayub Khan had enjoyed in his early years had long since faded. East Pakistan had revolted, was now Bangladesh. Cronyism infected his administration; kleptocrats and sycophants governed the provinces, controlled the lower courts.

We'd read about the marches in other cities. There would be a baton charge, then a gun charge, maybe the military would be called in. The morning after, a newspaper would print the body count, and the morning after that, it wouldn't print anything at all because the government had seized the presses. Three days later, the paper would reappear on the streets, a picture of Ayub Khan and his gleaming medals on the front page, and everyone was supposed to pretend it was still a free press.

The protesters were mostly students and lawyers, who were known as Black Coats because they wore their traditional legal uniforms into the streets. As a student, I was expected to join them. Bruises from batons were worn like combat ribbons, displayed with a warrior's pride, and hand-cuffs were trophies, held high above one's head, silver sparkling. To have no story to tell — of having pressed forward, of being nearly beaten, of eyes stung by tear gas — was to be a coward.

I was afraid. I watched from the side, close enough to convince myself I was part of the protest but far enough away to duck around a corner if the police started shooting. Knowing the protest was brewing, I'd left my bicycle at home that morning so it wouldn't get damaged in a melee or confiscated by the authorities.

Bodies lay in the street. Small swarms of police surrounded each one, batons rising, smashing down. They took big, sweeping kicks at the soft spots, the bellies and kidneys, and I watched bodies jerk, heard the thumps and moans. Blood leaked from noses, mouths, skulls; and when a person stopped moving, the police heaved him aside, like an animal carcass littering the street.

The crowd fell back, reassembled, flanked the police. "Baton charge!" Police pushed right, then left, and the crowd fell away again.

"Attention," the voice on the bullhorn said. "Section 144 has been imposed. Disperse immediately."

Section 144 had been a steady fear for years, a dark force always in the background. God forbid I should be out with three friends and a fourth joined us. Someone would have to leave. We'd all heard stories of young men rounded up for the crime of standing on a corner, stuffed into a vehicle and hauled away, or, if the police were in a hurry, simply shot.

I ran.

That evening, I told my parents what I'd seen.

"Why were you there?" my father wanted to know. He was not a fan of Khan, but he had little use for the opposition Pakistan People's Party, either. He thought Zulfikar Ali Bhutto was a fraud, a con man with an empty three-word promise for a slogan: *Roti, Kapra, Makan.* Bread, Clothing, Housing. (I was a supporter — I saw Bhutto rallying the masses to push aside an autocrat — but even I didn't believe he could deliver that much bread, let alone clothes and houses.) And my father had no tolerance for Bhutto's supporters shutting down the G.T.

Road and burning buses and smashing windows. "You shouldn't be anywhere near that sort of thing," he told me. "You know it's dangerous."

"I had to walk past it on my way —" I started to explain.

"You don't belong there," he said. For my father, for most people, it was easier to keep his head down, plow his fields, sow his wheat and sugarcane. "It is not your concern," he said.

I understood what he meant, that there is trouble one does not need to invite into his life. But what he didn't understand, what I was only beginning to understand, is that sometimes trouble happens in front of you, and you can't always turn away.

Two years later, I pulled a slim collection of poetry from a shelf deep in the stacks of Feroz Sons, a large yet still cramped and crowded bookstore east of the Old Campus in Lahore. My friend Farooq, who was studying English literature, had taken me there months before, walking up the Mall Road after class, past the posh restaurants on either side of a wide six-lane boulevard, past the old stone building that housed the High Court. I'd since wandered most of the aisles, settling in fiction some days, biography on another, history on still others.

I liked Feroz Sons because the clerks would let you stand near the shelves and read until your legs got tired and your lower back began to cramp and you had to walk outside and sit on a bench for a while, and they didn't mind when you came back in and started reading again. Maybe they assumed I was taking my time deciding what to buy, or perhaps they were just kind. I never bought anything. I couldn't afford books. I could afford to stand in the aisles. If I didn't have time to finish whatever I was reading, I'd make a note of what page I was on and slip it back into the stacks, but always three or four spots to one side or the other, hoping that might make it more difficult for a paying customer to take it home before I could finish.

I'd enrolled in law school in Lahore at the beginning of 1971. After I'd earned my bachelor's degree, family friends would ask my parents why I wasn't going to work, why I didn't get a job with the government or clerk in a shop, anything to help with the family. A college degree is more than enough, they'd say, more education than most people will ever have! That was not an unreasonable question, and the answer likely seemed an indulgence for a farmer's son: I went to law school because my grand-father's mantra — *No man is complete until his education is complete* — had soaked into my spirit, had become my mantra, too. Studying the law was a path to a respected profession, but more than that, it was a way for me to learn more, about the world, about people, about *anything.* For me, education was a quest.

Though he'd never gone to college, my father understood. He would nod and smile whenever those questions were asked. "It will all balance out," he would say. "In the end, it will all balance out." He was a calm, deliberate man with an abiding faith that life would always properly sort itself. Still, in private, he kept me in line. Whenever I would disagree with him about something — how long Ayub Khan would last, a particular way of eating a certain food, anything — he would say, "You can load a donkey with books, but that doesn't make him a scholar." I was, of course, the book-laden donkey. I had to earn the right to counter my elders.

My family scraped together the fees, a few dollars for tuition, a few more for a room in the dorms, and whenever I would visit them, my mother would slip a few bills into my pocket. I never looked to see how much she was handing me because I knew it was only a few rupees, five or ten. I didn't want to embarrass her, make her think I was disappointed it was so little, because I never was. It was enough to encourage me, money I knew she'd secreted away, money that wasn't going to one of my siblings, money I knew my father winked at her saving for me. I was always grateful.

But it was never enough to buy books. I had a hard enough time feeding myself. If the cafeteria was open, I could buy lentils for a penny or two that came with tandoori bread that was warm and wonderful and filling. If the cafeteria was closed, the man who sold tea from a wooden shack next to the dormitories would give me an egg sandwich on credit and a cup of tea for a penny. Tea was the anchor of my social life. There was another kiosk next to the law school, which had a big urn of hot water and loose tea and a pinch of cardamom that would steep all day into a strong brew. You could get a cup and saucer for a penny, fill it yourself from the tap, and sit on the immaculately manicured lawn, or under the shade of a neem tree. The tea seller's assistant darted about, collecting empty cups.

I read a lot of poetry at Feroz Sons. I was fond of the progressives and the literary

out to the ro
blooms in the v
the garden still
laid out like m

"Have you h
the United St
became a coun

We were you
perfectly accep

Farooq looke
said. Even Far
ture, hadn't
politics of the
were far more r
the Americans.

I told him a
how these peop
exactly — had
starting their c
selves from the
marized it as t
as we walked
cafeteria. Then
so he could rea

Farooq sat o
his back agai
absorbed the D
as he read. "Ye
"Yes! This is o

We talked ab

subversives, like Habib Jalib, or Qateel Shifai, who'd been imprisoned by Khan at one point. "Let me own," he wrote, "my unfulfilled desires." I recognized that as the powerful rebuke to tyranny that it was intended to be. He dedicated one of his volumes to "words that could not be published because of public violence."

The book I had now was a collection of Sahir Ludhianvi. I leafed through it and settled on a poem called "Taj Mahal." "The Taj, mayhap, to you may seem, a mark of love supreme," it began. "You may hold this beauteous vale in great esteem." Most people do. It was built by a Mughal emperor in 1632, a splendid white marble mausoleum on the bank of the Yamuna River to entomb one of his wives. It is often considered a memorial to eternal love. But is it? Is that what love requires, Ludhianvi was asking — outrageous wealth and quarried stone and a battalion of laborers? "Countless men in this world must have loved and gone / Who would say their loves weren't truthful or strong?"

The story of the subcontinent was one of plundered wealth, of shahs and emperors bathed in luxury yet surrounded by untold legions of impoverished and illiterate peasants. What if instead of a beautiful tomb, I

wondered, tl
bridge, an O
history have
serious quest
the alternativ
One's feeling
crude litmus
monument o
to equal dig
entitled to m
"An emper
Has played v
wrote. "Mee
other place."
I was a stu
about the p
about the sti
desperate to
place.

I read the De
and over an
room, until
crawled up tl
fascinated, e
hundred yea
sleeping part
Like a con
to share it.
A day or s

rose garden and then, when the weather warmed, under the neem trees, moving around the trunks with the sun to stay in the shade of the canopies. His English was better than mine, and he helped me understand some of the more arcane words and phrases, that *kindred* and *brethren* meant they were declaring independence from their own people.

We also wondered about colonialism, whether any creatures other than humans inflicted such unmitigated savagery on their own kind. We agreed the Constitution itself was rather dry, but we marveled at the amendments. Freedom of assembly? How wondrous to have such a thing! Freedom of speech? Our professors who'd been educated in England had told us about Speakers' Corner, a spot in one of London's big green parks where anyone could say anything about anyone. It had always seemed fantastical, but here it was, codified into law. And just the first five words of the First Amendment were a majestic oddity: *Congress shall make no law* . . . . The other constitutions I'd studied were written wholly in the affirmative — Parliament can do this, the prime minister can do that — but here were people standing up to tyrants and saying, explicitly, that there were certain things their government could *not* do, freedoms that could not ever be taken away. There was an immediate sense of power curtailed, of actions preemptively precluded. And then there was the Fourteenth Amendment, my favorite, guaranteeing equal protection to everyone, not just to the favored classes or to the people who could afford to bend the law to their will. The very fact that there were amendments was magnificent: The rules could be modified to more ably and comprehensively serve the good of the people, as if the document itself was alive, reactive, adaptive.

Such revelations led to more complicated questions about our own autonomy. Pakistan was a sovereign nation by another's decree, borders drawn by a foreign power, millions of people displaced when a line on a map separated India and Pakistan. What if the people had claimed their own destiny? Why hadn't we declared our independence? Were our leaders not bold enough, not bright enough? Had we been made meek by generations of subjugation? Our forefathers had tried to rebel once, peasants and tradesmen rising up in 1857 against British rule, a hundred thousand of them slaughtered for their trouble. The subcontinent had been taken over, exploited, plundered, by the

East India Trading Company, a handful of businessmen who'd pitted emperor against maharajah. Why hadn't we stood up to them?

Farooq and I never answered that question. Untangling the threads of history is never easy. Maybe there was no simple answer for what had been. But we knew what could be. We knew what was possible.

CHAPTER 2
TWENTY-ONE SPARROWS

One day in the winter of 1972, I was summoned to the office of Wazir-ul-Hasan Abdi. This was curious: I knew who Abdi was, the director of the Persian Studies program, which was in the prestigious Oriental College, an ornate red brick building with minarets at the corners and a second-floor balcony stretching across the front. I passed it every day, as it was directly opposite the identical structure where the Punjab University Law College was housed, two distinguished institutions mirroring each other across a wide and manicured green shaded by neem trees and trimmed with roses. The university had pristine grounds, a sanctuary from the rest of Lahore, a dusty, gritty sprawl of nearly two million people.

I had no classes in the Oriental College, no business with Abdi. I found it curious that he would want to see me, but not unnerving. His office was on the first floor. I knocked, bade him *salaam*. "You wanted to see me?"

"Yes, please, come sit," Abdi said, motioning toward a plain chair near his desk. He had a thin face and a fuzz of short white hair, and he seemed an affable man, serious in his manners but not in himself. I noticed the books crowding the shelves; from the bindings and gold embossing, they looked expensive and important, a learned professor's treasures.

"I asked to see you," Abdi said, "because we are having an event next week, a reception for the ambassador from Iran, and I would like you to come."

Abdi was speaking in Urdu. In the next breath, unannounced and abruptly, he switched to Farsi. "I hear that you speak very good Farsi."

"I love Farsi," I answered, by reflex, in Farsi.

"Bah! Bah!" he said. He clapped his hands together, giddy. "Wow! Wow. How do you speak so well?"

It was true that I spoke Farsi fluently, colloquially, and with the neutral accent of a Tehran native. My grandfather had put the rhythm and lilt of Farsi in my ears many years ago, reading Rumi at the foot of my cot, and the basics had seeped into my memory. On the second floor of my dorm and part of the third, there were students from Persia, some of whom wanted to improve their English. One in particular, a Tehranian named Shams, asked me to practice with him. "Look at this," he said after months of talking in both languages. "I've come to you to learn English, and I've taught you Farsi." In time, I became well known on campus as the Pakistani student who could speak coherently and easily with the Persian ones. But to be asked to greet an ambassador was a high honor, one I readily accepted.

The reception was held in the faculty lounge, a plush, almost ornate room in the Oriental College, the floor covered here and there with beautiful Persian rugs, the windows flanked by long, thick curtains tied back with golden ropes. The ostensible purpose was to impress the ambassador, whose country offered a generous amount of support to the Persian Studies department, so it was scheduled for the afternoon, in order to allow female students to attend, show off their language skills, and still catch a bus back to the dorms on New Campus before nightfall.

I arrived early, greeted Abdi, introduced myself to the other professors. I wore a suit jacket and a white turtleneck, and might easily have been mistaken for a young professor by students who didn't know me, which would include everyone studying Persian.

The senior students arrived, and they spoke in a mixture of Urdu and English and stilted, academic Farsi. The younger students filed in next. Most of them wore *shalwar kameez,* except for one woman who was dressed in a pale yellow sari. I noticed only that she had fair skin and light brown hair — but little else, because I did not let my gaze linger. To do so, in that time and that place, would have been impolite. When I walked around campus, I kept my eyes down, watching the ground passing beneath me, as a matter of habit and general respect to those around me. Women were not to be ogled, even briefly.

The students made small talk with the ambassador. I had a brief conversation with him about nothing important, though he did compliment my fluency and accent. Then we all sat and the woman in the yellow sari brought a tray of tea. That, I realized, was why she was dressed so nicely: She had been selected to serve the ambassador. She carried the tray toward him, but she offered it first to Abdi, the head of her

60

department. That was a sign of great respect. An ambassador may have a more impressive title, but to a student, the head of her department is more important. Other than noticing that small gesture, though, I did not pay any more attention to the woman serving tea.

The woman in the yellow sari was Ghazala Durrani. Her name, had I known it, would not have made a startling impression upon me, but it means, roughly, "pearl of the ages." It comes from Ahmad Shah Durrani, who is considered the father of modern Afghanistan and of whom Ghazala is a direct eighth-generation descendant. In the eighteenth century, Ahmad Shah united tribes around Kandahar into a confederation and then, after conquering Mughals and others, spread his empire east to Delhi, west into what is now Iran and Turkmenistan, and south to the Arabian Sea.

In the raiding and looting common to any expanding empire, Ahmad Shah Durrani happened to come into possession of the Koh-i-Noor, a massive 125-carat diamond believed to have been dug out of an Indian mine thousands of years earlier. The stone — whose name means "mountain of light" — stayed with the family for decades, passed down through sons and grandsons, shifting from one to another as cousins and brothers took to imprisoning and blinding and occasionally killing one another in struggles for power and wealth. Eventually, the stone passed to Shah Shujah Durrani, Ghazala's great-great-great-grandfather.

There are several versions of the story of what happened to the Koh-i-Noor. The one accepted by Ghazala's family and some historians is that Shah Shujah had smuggled the stone out of Afghanistan in his turban when he fled a family feud. He went to Punjab, where the local Sikh king in Lahore, Ranjit Singh, learned of the diamond, either through rumors or spies. He arranged a formal state ceremony to welcome Shah Shujah, inviting all the local dignitaries. In front of all the important people, he told Shah Shujah that they were now brothers, and that they should exchange turbans as a sign of their kinship, a common ritual. Ranjit Singh removed his and held it out for Shah Shujah. What could he do? Publicly refuse an offer of friendship, humiliate his host?

He gave Singh his turban. Singh, in turn, gave the diamond to the British to curry favor, and the British sent it to Queen Victoria, who set it into the front of her crown.

It is now on display in the Tower of London with the rest of the Crown Jewels.

Ghazala grew up beneath the portraits of all the great Durrani rulers of the past, hung on the wall of the sitting room: Ahmad Shah, Shah Zaman, Shah Shujah, and so on. The extended family, cousins and uncles, used to verbally annotate them, argue about who had a straighter, purer line back to Ahmad Shah. Ghazala's family had good claim: Both of her parents could trace their lineage directly to Ahmad Shah. That side of the family had long before settled in Ludhiana, in what is now India, where they lived the prosperous life of exiled royalty.

Among those portraits on the wall was one of Shah Shujah's son, Nadir Shah Durrani, who was a poet of some renown. That's why Ghazala was in Lahore, in the Persian Studies department, working on her master's degree. Her thesis was on her great-great-grandfather, as if she was excavating and exploring her past through his poetry.

After partition in 1947, Ghazala's branch of the Durranis migrated across the border to Pakistan with the rest of the Muslim majority. They left everything behind, their homes and land, and eventually applied to the government relocation office for equivalent replacements. Their request was approved, but "equivalent" is a malleable word. The Durranis were by no means impoverished, but no longer were they royalty, either.

Her family was in fact quite well off, for in a young country ruled by an autocrat, connections matter, and her family was connected: One of her father's brothers (he had five) had been a college roommate of Ayub Khan, and her maternal uncle was the head of Khan's civil defense apparatus.

Her father was a land commissioner, responsible for collecting property taxes and approving property transfers and the like. It was a civil service job, but a prized one, almost designed for kickbacks and shaving acres from prospective sales. *Oh, you would like to buy five hundred hectares? I will need one hundred of them, in my cousin's name, please.* There was a bitterly told joke in Pakistan about a governor who takes his wife to dinner at the local land commissioner's home. She gapes at their host's ostentatious wealth. "Why do you waste your time being governor?" she says to her husband. "You should be the land commissioner!"

Ghazala's father, Amin-u-Din Durrani, bore no resemblance to that joke. He was an honest man and a proper public servant.

People, including his wife, would ask sometimes why he didn't acquire more land, more rupees, riches he could pass to his children. "You have to lie in your grave," he would answer, "and I have to lie in mine." He made a comfortable living, owned a house with two stories and electricity and water that flowed from a tank municipal workers pumped full every so often, and could afford a servant to clean the house and another to cook the meals. He would lie comfortably in his grave, as he did in his bed.

He had four children, two girls and two boys, of whom Ghazala was the eldest. He adored her. *"Chashm e maan dunbaalish,"* he used to say. "Wherever she goes, my eye follows. She brings comfort to my eyes." He was protective, as all fathers are, and it was difficult for him to let her wander too far from his gaze. From a young age, Ghazala was the key shooter on a netball team — it's like basketball without the backboard — and eventually would captain championship teams in college. In seventh grade, her team was invited to an out-of-town tournament, only a hundred miles away and only for a couple of nights. Her father refused to let her go. "During the day, fine," he said. "But you sleep here at night." The coach pleaded,

65

promised that the adult women were responsible, would keep a close eye on all the girls. "There is no team without a shooter," she said. Her father relented, and he grew more comfortable with it each year. "So, where are you going this year?" he would ask as tournament season came closer.

She was a serious student, fond of literature and Persian — which the family still spoke at home — yet gifted in the sciences, too. Her high school principal told her mother that Ghazala should go to medical school. Her mother appreciated the confidence, but, unfortunately, Ghazala couldn't stand the sight of blood.

When she wasn't in school, she would learn practical skills, sewing and embroidery and baking. She became quite adept at making her own clothes, but she never took to baking, as it meant spending too much time in the kitchen.

She graduated from college in Faisalabad with a degree in philosophy and Persian. And then she came to Lahore to write a master's thesis on her great-great-grandfather the poet.

But of course I knew none of that then, and wouldn't know all of it for many years. I just knew her as a student chosen to serve tea to the ambassador.

■ ■ ■ ■

A few days after the reception with the ambassador, I saw the woman who'd worn the yellow sari coming down a staircase in the Oriental College. I was going up, to the second floor, the balcony, to chant political slogans. The beginning of the academic year was campaign season for the student union, and it was quite boisterous. This was student politics, completely divorced from what was happening in the streets, and our issues were not of shattering importance — running the buses more frequently was a popular demand. But at the time they seemed a worthwhile diversion, exercising what little political muscle we had. I was aligned with the Green Party, which represented nothing more significant than a color opposite that of our opponents, the Red Party (though the Reds did in fact have a decided Marxist tilt). Also, green was economical. We couldn't afford proper banners and flags, so before every rally a few of us would scamper up trees — only city trees, never the ones on campus — and break off leafy branches we could wave instead.

After class, we would meet on the lawn between the law college and the Oriental

College and chant at each other. There was always more green than red coloring the crowd — red-leafed trees were scarce to nonexistent in Lahore — and our chants were loud and sincere and rather insipid. *Green is the color of the future* would be answered by *Red is the color of the future. The world is green! The world is red! Vote green! Vote red!* Students would watch from the balconies, unless we decided, as I had that day, to yell our slogans from above and let others listen from below.

The woman who served tea passed me in the middle of a flight. I recognized her fair skin, her light brown hair. I noticed she had green eyes.

She was stunningly beautiful.

"Hello, sir," she said as she passed me going down.

"Hello," I answered, and kept climbing.

Sir? She'd called me sir. She thought I was a professor.

I saw her again not long after that on the bus from Old Campus, where the academic buildings stood, to New Campus, where the dormitories were located. She was in the front with the women and I was in the back where the men always sat, but I could see her light hair, her fair skin, her green eyes.

68

The bus stopped first at Hostel 1, a square, modern building three stories tall, identical to Hostel 2 and Hostel 3, where I lived.

I watched her walk away from the bus. I was intrigued. Not smitten, exactly, but curious. The problem was that a man — a gentleman — couldn't simply approach a woman, couldn't say hello for no reason at all, certainly couldn't directly ask to have dinner or go to a movie (neither of which I could afford, anyway). One needed either to be introduced or to have a pretext — an accidentally convenient reason — to speak.

Finding one would be difficult. But a few days later, as I waited for the bus on Old Campus, I saw her walking toward the stop, two or three friends with her. It was purely happenstance, the two of us in proximity again.

I didn't want to miss the bus, but I didn't want to miss my chance, either.

My feet started moving, one step, then another, away from the bus stop, toward the woman who'd worn the yellow sari. I looked at the ground.

The gap closed. We were ten feet away, six, two.

I looked up. "Hello," I said.

"Hello," she said.

Neither of us broke our pace. We passed quickly, fleetingly. Neither of us had smiled.

Falling in love was a laborious process in Pakistan in the 1970s. Without friends or family to make a proper introduction, I was forced to work the margins, circling in slowly from a distance. To be aggressive would have been disrespectful, and that would have been a fatal tactical error. Worse, this was all new to me. I'd never had a girlfriend or even dated before, which was not uncommon for a young man in those days. There had been no sexual revolution in Pakistan; there had not been even a minor insurrection.

I wasn't even sure what I was feeling. Longing? Desire? Infatuation?

I had managed to learn her name — Ghazala — by making it a point to canvass for the Greens at the Oriental College. She was with friends, but we all introduced ourselves. I told them I hoped they would vote Green. Had we discussed serious politics — had she told me then, as I later learned, that she believed Bhutto was ruining the modern country Ayub Khan had built — maybe I would have lost interest. But that would have been a much too intimate conversation. Perhaps there is something to be said for the old ways of decorum.

She was obviously intelligent, given that she was studying for her master's degree. The only other things I knew were where she lived and that she rode the bus.

I worked with what I had. My first class began at 9:30, so I took the bus that left the front of Hostel 3 at nine o'clock, then stopped at Hostels 2 and 1 before continuing to Old Campus, the reverse of the route that would bring us back. I got on in the back, as was customary, but found a seat near the middle, sitting as close to the front as I could so I could see if she boarded.

At Hostel 1, Ghazala did not get on.

The next morning, I took the eight o'clock bus. She did not get on that one, either.

I took the seven o'clock bus on the third day. She got on. I did not say anything, and I did not look at her for long. But I took the seven o'clock every morning after.

In the afternoons, I waited to take the two o'clock bus back, because I'd figured out she would be on it. Some days, if I watched carefully from the lawn at the corner of the law school building, I could see her walking toward the bus stop, and if she was alone I would start walking, too, timing my steps to intersect with hers. We would say hello and

I might ask her mundane questions — *How are you settling into the dorms? Is your thesis going well?* — the smallest of small talk.

But for me, it was thrilling.

This went on for more than a month, me riding early buses and late buses, hoping just to glimpse her and perhaps speak a few ostentatiously neutral words. Weekends became torture, because there was no reason to pass her, to glimpse her even from a distance. I couldn't go to her dorm — there was a guard at the door, visitors had to be expected, and, in any case, to be so forward would have been mortifying for both of us. Occasionally, she wouldn't be on the Monday morning bus because, I later learned, she'd spent the weekend with her parents and they'd dropped her at Old Campus. On those days, I'd suffer a flutter of panic until I saw her in the afternoon.

Winter eased into spring. Between the hostels, there was a cafeteria and a laundry and a row of shops that sold ice cream and incidentals and such. I happened to be there one afternoon, at the end closest to Ghazala's dorm, when she happened to be with some friends at the opposite end. And we were walking toward each other.

I decided I would approach her more deliberately. I decided I would be direct.

Please, I thought to myself, *let nothing disrespectful come out of my mouth.*

"Ghazala," I said when we were close enough, "may I speak with you?"

She stopped, smiled. "Yes, I suppose so." I hoped my relief wasn't too obvious. If she had said no, I would have been crushed. Even such an innocuous request was heavily freighted. Her friends, who kindly continued walking, understood right away. "Oh, he likes you," they told her later. "Don't you see him, walking around campus? He never looks at girls. He wouldn't ask to speak with you if he didn't like you."

We spoke of nothing complicated or especially personal; neither of us, in fact, remembers the substance of the conversation now. But she had not *declined* to talk to me, which meant she had not rejected me. On the other hand, it also meant no more than that. But I would take what I could get.

The following Friday, I saw her at the bus stop and decided to take things further. "Hello, Ghazala," I said. I tried to keep my voice steady, nonchalant. "I was wondering, may I speak with you tomorrow?"

She smiled. "Sure," she said. "Come in the afternoon."

This was tremendous progress. We had arranged a meeting. Not a date, exactly, but a scheduled time to talk. She would have to leave word with the guard that I was expected. She was affirmatively and publicly accepting my presence.

It did not occur to me that she, too, was nervous.

I went to her dormitory the next day. The guard announced me and she came down. We walked through the gardens nearby, and then I invited her to have tea at the cafeteria. I talked about student politics, told her there was going to be a musical procession — the Greens very much wanted a music department at the university — and imagined how funny it was going to be to see the harmonium players lugging their big, boxy keyboards at the front of the march. She told me she was from Faisalabad, that she was writing her thesis about a poet who was the son of Shah Shujah, that she planned to be a professor of Persian once she completed her degree.

She did not tell me that she used to carry a stick around campus in Faisalabad, a symbol of Ayub Khan's authority. She did not declare, as she would later, "Ayub Khan brought electricity to Pakistan," which was true but, to my mind, beside the point. That was not, in hindsight, unusual. She was raised in a family that, by dint of history and connections and social standing, supported Ayub Khan; it was what she knew, the context in which she'd been raised. To draw an American comparison, it was not unlike a young woman born to Eisenhower parents voting Republican. Still, it was probably for the best that it wasn't mentioned just then.

I was falling in love, slowly but most assuredly. Every so often, I would sneak a glance around the cafeteria. I wanted to see who was there. No, I wanted to know who saw *us* there, together, Muazzam and Ghazala. And when we left, I walked as slowly as I could without being awkward. I wanted to make sure we were seen by as many people as possible, that students of New Campus would know that this exquisite young lady already had a suitor.

One evening in late spring, Professor Abdi asked Ghazala and me to be on a Persian-language radio show with him. There did not appear to be any pretext to the invitation. The topic was intercultural influences, the entwining and complementing of various languages and cultures. So far as I knew, we just happened to be the two students most fluent in Persian.

75

We went to the studio together, Ghazala, Abdi, and I, and the three of us took a taxi from the studio back to New Campus when it was over. Ghazala and I again made small talk, nothing of any consequence. But Abdi was older and wiser and had a finely tuned antenna. A few days afterward, he summoned me again to his office.

"It's very rare," he told me, "to have a student with her background."

I nodded noncommittally, unsure what he meant.

"You don't know who her family is, do you?"

I shook my head. "No, sir."

Abdi told me Ghazala's entire lineage, from Ahmad Shah Durrani, the last emperor of Afghanistan and a poet Iqbal himself had called "an everlasting brook," through Shah Shujah and the Koh-i-Noor, to Shujah's eldest son, the poet about whom Ghazala was writing her thesis. Abdi explained to me, in other words, that I was courting royalty.

Ghazala had told me she was writing a thesis. She'd never mentioned any of the rest.

My friend Afzal and I got off the bus from Gujranwala in Faisalabad, found a rickshaw, and told the driver to take us to 224 People's Colony. I held a book in my lap, making sure I didn't scuff the cover or bend any of the pages. There was nothing special about the book, only that it was hers, one that I'd seen her carrying, one that I knew she'd have when I asked to borrow it.

Admittedly, it was a clumsy ploy. There was more unrest in the streets, students and Black Coats marching against something or other, maybe a disputed election or a random edict or a general injustice, perceived or real. The reason wasn't important enough for me to remember years later, as civil disturbances were not uncommon in the early 1970s. What mattered to me was that the government, as a matter of course, responded by shutting down the universities and dispersing the students. The campuses might be closed for a week, but just as often for two or three, even a month. So before all the students in Lahore were sent home, I'd asked Ghazala for a book. I had no intention of reading it, and I can't now even recall what it was. But at the very least, returning it would give me an excuse to see her once the university reopened.

I lasted one agonizing week before I begged Afzal to go with me to Faisalabad. A young man showing up alone on Ghazala's doorstep, even to return a book, would have been far too aggressive. But if there were two of us, well scrubbed and neatly dressed, that would seem relatively innocent and not wholly transparent.

The rickshaw driver took us through a large gate into Ghazala's neighborhood. There was a park in front of her family's house, which was two stories tall with a water tank. My heart was pounding. "Relax," Afzal said. "Deep breaths. You need to relax."

We knocked on the front door. A teen-aged boy, Ghazala's youngest brother, answered. I stammered an introduction, said I was there to return a book she might need for her studies. What could be more proper and harmless?

The boy nodded and disappeared inside. I heard him call for Ghazala, but nothing else. Apparently, he'd told her we were there, and why. I learned later that she was partly annoyed and partly embarrassed — not that I was there, but that I was still standing on the doorstep. "And you left them outside?" Ghazala whispered to her brother. "Invite them in! Keep them in the living room."

The rest was only mildly awkward. Ghazala smiled when she saw me, thanked me for the book she didn't really need. Her mother greeted us warmly, these two polite students so concerned with her daughter's studies. Her father, a soft-spoken and well-fed man who, however, didn't look as if he'd already suffered two heart attacks, insisted we stay for lunch, considering we'd traveled for more than three hours to get there. They served us Afghani pilau, a dish of rice browned with onions and mixed with spices and diced chicken, and Shami kebabs and spinach and curried chicken, a wonderful feast. If they noticed my infatuation with Ghazala, they did not let on; we were treated with the generous hospitality afforded any respectable guest, no more and no less.

Then we got on a bus back to Gujranwala, where I would wait another dreadfully long week.

When the university reopened, I went to Ghazala's dormitory the morning I returned. The guard told me she hadn't come back yet. I went to class, walked around campus, did anything to occupy my time. I waited as long as I could before I went back. I hoped the shift had changed, that a new guard would be at the hostel.

The shift had not changed. "Why do you come twice in one day?" he asked me. "I will tell her you've come."

I blushed. "Thank you," I said. "It's just that . . . that I have some books to return to her. I think they're very, um, important."

I had no books, of course. I'd already used that ruse. But there was nothing more crucial in that moment than seeing Ghazala. Those weeks away from campus, I didn't miss my professors, didn't long for my textbooks, didn't daydream of new chants for the Greens. I thought only of Ghazala. The mechanics might differ from place to place, culture to culture, but love is a universal force, like gravity. It pulls you in, and then you're tumbling, falling head over heels and all the other clichés, until a splendid dizziness blurs your thoughts, fuzzes everything on the periphery, and all you can see, clear and sharp, is that one person, that one desire.

Walking away from her dorm was agony. I would have to check the schedule, figure out when a new guard would come on duty before I tried again.

"I want you to meet her," I said in the spring. "I want you to come to Lahore and spend the day with her."

My mother clapped her hands together, let out a giddy laugh. "Oh, Muazzam," she said. "This is wonderful. Tell me about her.

Tell me!"

I had never asked my mother to meet a woman before. I'd never, in fact, mentioned a woman before. So she understood I wasn't asking her to pay a courtesy visit to a casual friend. At the same time, Ghazala understood I wasn't merely suggesting she might enjoy a brief lunch with my mother, no matter how mightily I tried to sound casual. I hadn't asked her to marry me — my parents would have to do that — but I had clearly signaled my intentions. Had she declined, I would have been devastated. Instead, she happily agreed, and then poured nervous energy into scrubbing her room.

But what could I tell my mother about her? That she was beautiful and intelligent and modest? That I would go to her dorm in the evenings when the moon was full and fat and ask her to walk in the gardens and stare up at the sky with me? That she loved the potato patties served with a chutney of peppermint, green chiles, and tamarind that one of the vendors at old Anarkali fried in a giant wok? That she was an Afghani princess?

I'm pretty sure I left that last part out.

There was little to worry about. My mother and her closest confidante, my eldest sister, came to Lahore in the late spring and spent a day with Ghazala. I was not with them, as that would have been improper. But I was delighted to hear that they adored her, and she them. Before they left, my mother hugged her.

One side, my side, was delighted.

A month or two later, Ghazala led her mother into the small room near the front door of her dormitory, a space usually used by students to talk, as men weren't allowed farther inside. She was a graceful woman, impeccably dressed, a little taller than her daughter with hair several shades darker.

She reminded me of my grandmother. There was no physical resemblance — my grandmother had a fair complexion and long white hair she often gathered into a ponytail — but they both had *presence,* a dignity that radiated from them, a nearly physical force that filled a room. "You don't judge the dignity of a house by how big the car outside is," my grandmother used to tell me. "You judge it by the dignity of the women inside."

My grandmother was a kind woman, always tender and smelling faintly of roses, but she was firm. If food was on the table but a child — me — needed to be disciplined, to have a lesson explained, the meal would always wait. She believed there was no more important duty for a parent, or grandparent, than to properly raise a child, because that child would have children, and those children would have children, and on through the generations. She wasn't raising one child, then, but contributing to an endless, eternal community.

Ghazala delivered her mother, then left us alone to talk. I waited for her mother to sit, then settled into a chair. Ghazala's parents had come to see her, and had met a day or two before with Professor Abdi at his request. After talking about her thesis, Abdi had asked Ghazala to get the three of them some water. She stepped out of the room, leaving Abdi with her parents.

"There is a very nice young man who would be perfect for Ghazala," Abdi quickly told them. "His name is Muazzam Khan, a law student. You should look into him."

Her mother tried to find out more about me from Ghazala, but she was too embarrassed to answer, so a friend told her the basics, not much more than what Abdi already had said. Her mother then asked Ghazala — which, in context, was more of a command than a request — to meet me, which is why Ghazala had arranged for both of us, her mother and me, to be in that small room on a summer afternoon.

Her mother was businesslike, not unfriendly but not solicitous, either. This was a serious matter, a young man pursuing her daughter. She had already identified a potential groom for Ghazala, a cousin with a large house and many acres of land and a career in the military, the most prestigious profession in Pakistan. Marriage was not a romantic coupling of two people but the commingling of two entire families. The priority wasn't necessarily Ghazala's happiness but her comfort, whether she would be provided for in a suitable manner. My family, lower middle class, was several steps below hers. I knew that in a traditional sense, I was a wholly unsuitable groom. Whether I approved of that tradition was immaterial. I understood it, and that was enough.

"Tell me about your family," she said.

"There are ten of us," I said. "I am the eldest of five sons and five daughters."

"What are your plans?"

"I will complete my law degree next year and be licensed and then I will practice law, *inshallah.*"

"And what do your parents do?"

"They are farmers."

"How much land do they have?"

I honestly did not know. I'd never counted the acres or measured the perimeter, nor heard my father ever say how big the fields of wheat and sugarcane were. But she wasn't looking for a precise answer.

"We are modest people," I said. "It is a modest farm, and I come from humble means."

She didn't really respond to that. What could she say? It was nobody's fault, just the way our part of the world worked.

"He is a fine young man, Ghazala. But what can he offer you?"

Ghazala was in Faisalabad with her parents during the short summer break.

"What does he have?" Ghazala's mother asked her at home. "What can he give you, how can he take care of you?"

"He's going to be a lawyer —"

"A lawyer!" Her mother cut her off. "Lawyers are a dime a dozen! What do they do except have marches and get beaten in the streets?"

Ghazala was silent. It was true that while lawyers were held in some regard, the young ones did spend an uncomfortable amount of time protesting and getting clubbed in baton charges.

"Your cousin has land and a house. He

has prestige. He will make a fine husband."

Ghazala was in an impossible situation. She couldn't defy her mother, but neither could she deny her affection for me. In frustration, she told me later, she lashed out. "Fine," she said, in a tone she'd never taken with her mother before. "If that's what you want for me, I will do it. But I will pray, I *have* prayed, that Muazzam will become president. And then you will see. Then you will see I should have married him."

She stormed off. Her mother was taken aback, but she believed the episode would pass. Ghazala, in her eyes, was still a child. She didn't know what was best for herself.

Ghazala turned twenty-one at the end of August 1972. But what gift could I possibly give her? She had many small luxuries and all the reasonable comforts money could buy, and I had very little money to spend. I still owed the tea seller money for egg sandwiches. And what if I'd had money? Any present I gave her, she would have to explain to her parents. She was already defying her mother by not rejecting me out of hand. I needed a gift that would show her what was in my heart, rather than my pockets.

The gift I decided on was simple. I wrapped it in newspaper, a cube about the size of a large microwave oven, but light enough to carry with one hand if I chose to. I carried it from my dormitory to hers, along the sidewalk where I'd first worked up the nerve to speak to her. I gave it to the guard at the front door, and left before he called Ghazala. Lingering after arriving unannounced would have been inappropriate. What if there was an embarrassing scene, this impoverished student pestering Ghazala with his feeble gift?

That would pass. I knew that once Ghazala saw what was inside, she would understand immediately, both the significance of the gift and the depth of my love for her.

Ghazala came down. Three of her friends had followed her, a gift left by a young man being a reason for all manner of curiosity. She told me later how she lifted the package and felt it wiggle, as if something inside was moving. Startled, she set it down quickly and stepped back. What was this? She wondered if perhaps I was playing a trick on her, that maybe I'd wrapped up a cat or some other small creature that would jump out at her. She stared at it for a moment before reaching out her right hand, stretching it as far from her body as possible, and gingerly squeezing with the tips of her fingers the handle I'd left poking up through the newspaper. She carried it like that, as if it might detonate, just inside the door and set it down in the corridor, close to the wall.

"You open it," Ghazala said to one of her friends. "Please, you open it. I'm afraid." She giggled nervously.

Her friend gently peeled back one corner of the newspaper. She let out a faint, delighted gasp.

"Oh!" she said. "You don't know what he's done, do you?"

Ghazala shook her head.

"You don't know how beautiful this is . . ."

Her friend pulled away more of the paper. There was a wire cage beneath it and, inside the cage, twenty-one gray sparrows.

I'd bought them at Tollinton Market. I would have preferred white doves, but those were five rupees each; sparrows were the least expensive bird in the market. And the point was the same. Islam teaches that the Creator made nothing in a cage, and that to release one of His creations back into the wild was an act of kindness and mercy.

Ghazala smiled. Her lip trembled.

I knew she would understand.

"Look, he's left you a note."

Ghazala took the folded sheet I'd tucked into the wires of the cage. *Release these at dawn,* I'd written, *and from wherever they fly, they will send you great blessings.*

Her eyes grew wet with tears she tried to blink away. That was the moment, she told me many years later, that she knew she loved me, too.

All of her friends, which was almost everyone in Hostel 1, lined up outside Ghazala's door just before dawn the next morning. They went out onto the balcony. Some of the women said their morning prayers as the blue-black of the eastern sky melted into a deep crimson veined with pink.

Ghazala slid open the door of the cage. The sparrows hopped, tentative, curious, until one made it through the opening, then another, and finally there appeared a flurry of tiny gray wings, twenty-one sparrows flittering up into the rising sun.

Chapter 3
A Stick Becomes a Ney

I walked to the other side of the canal bisecting New Campus in the late afternoon, past the academic buildings toward a row of tidy bungalows where the professors lived. The physical terrain was familiar, but I was wandering into uncharted territory, filled with a despairing dread that, through a prayer whispered to myself, I'd alchemized into an anxious hope.

My formal legal studies were behind me by the late spring of 1973. The only requirements remaining before I could receive my law license were to pass a final exam and complete a nine-month apprenticeship with a senior lawyer. The problem was, I had to take the exam before I could start my apprenticeship, and the exam required a fee, which I didn't have. I was still buying egg sandwiches on credit, and I owed the cafeteria for meals, too.

The exam was to be given the next morning. My future — would I be a lawyer or a failure? — would be determined in the next few hours.

I'd already gone to my parents for help. I'd taken the bus to Gujranwala a few days earlier, a knot in my stomach. Their friends continued to wonder why I wasn't working, why their oldest son wasn't earning enough to help support his family. Law school was an imposition on my parents; every rupee my mother had slipped into my pocket was a rupee that wasn't spent on my siblings, and there were only so many rupees to go around. I knew there wasn't a secret stash set aside for emergencies, let alone exam fees. Just asking would be placing another burden upon them, would make my hardship their hardship, my struggle their struggle. But where else could I turn?

We sat in their bedroom. I explained that the deadline for filing my exam application was approaching. I could reserve a seat by sending in the paperwork, but I wouldn't be allowed to take the test, or get my results, until the fee was paid.

"How much is the fee?" my father asked.

I looked at the floor. "Two hundred and thirty rupees."

"Two hundred and thirty rupees!" he said. "You know we don't have that kind of money."

I gave a slight, embarrassed nod.

"How are you going to pay for it?" he asked.

"That's why I'm here," I said.

"Can you pay part of it now, and more later, when you have a job?"

I shook my head.

There was a painful silence.

"We just don't have the money," my father said.

My mother, always my advocate, said I had to take the exam. If I waited until I had the money, if I delayed it a year, that year might turn into two, and then three, and then forever. And I was prepared now, right? I'd studied, was confident I would do well?

"Yes, yes," I said. "I'm sure I'd do very well."

She turned to my father. "We can't let him not finish, not when he is so close," she said. She turned to me. "Go ahead and file the papers, and God will provide a way."

The irony was, I was entirely ambivalent about actually *being* a lawyer. I'd enrolled in law school not as a calculated prelude to a career but out of intellectual curiosity and idealism.

No man is complete until his education is complete.

I had no interest in the hard sciences or in being a physician. Law, on the other hand, would teach me more about society — about the way the rules of civilization are developed and codified, about liberty and the lack thereof, about the way people organized themselves into a functioning body politic — than any other subject. Law school was a prism through which I could study my true interest, the human condition.

That was the intellectual part. The idealism sprang from the long history of lawyers in progressive social movements, both in modern Pakistan and in the colonized subcontinent. The founder of Pakistan, Muhammad Ali Jinnah, was a brilliant, British-educated attorney. Mahatma Gandhi had been trained as a lawyer. So had Bhutto, who'd been elected president in 1971. Ghazala's mother was correct: Lawyers did spend a lot of time parading and getting beaten in the streets. Black Coats led the marches in Karachi and Rawalpindi and Lahore and all the other cities; when I first saw people clubbed to the pavement in Gujranwala, Black Coats were the ones beaten down first.

I had no desire to be beaten. But Black Coats had defied martial law and helped drive Khan from power. Black Coats marched for Bhutto and against a rising Islamist movement. I never believed Bhutto could deliver on his promises, but I was always for the people over the autocrats and theocrats. And that practical idealism was embedded in the academic community, the activism nurtured by faculty. After every protest — for workers' rights or freer elections or a new constitution — a professor named Nazir Ahmed would pedal his bicycle to the police stations, the basket bolted to the handlebars stuffed with naan and lentils. "These are my students you've arrested," he'd plead with the officers. "Please, at least let them eat."

How that idealism would translate into action for me was still unclear. But at least I'd figured out which side I was on: that of the oppressed masses against the entrenched few who wielded ruthless power.

For all that, though, I knew a young lawyer would earn a laborer's wages. It was a prestigious profession; in a country where more than 95 percent of the population was illiterate, the local attorney was held in the same regard as the village doctor. Who else would organize contracts and settle disputes and guide people through a byzantine bureaucracy? But poor people don't have much to pay beyond their respect. As a general rule, it took years, and often an advanced degree from England, for a lawyer to work his way up to the wealthy clients who could afford reasonable fees. I would have an easier time supporting Ghazala as a shopkeeper.

Still, law was the path I'd chosen. I couldn't move forward without my license, and I couldn't get my license until I'd passed, and paid for, the exam. Except now it was the night before the test, and God had not provided two hundred and thirty rupees. As I walked across the canal, nervousness mingled with a touch of shame. How could I do this to my family, stumbling just short of the finish line after all my parents had invested? How could I face my brothers and sisters — the eldest son, the one they looked up to, now just an example of incomplete goals, unrealized dreams?

Worse than all that, the thought of disappointing Ghazala was crushing. Her mother had warmed to me, but she was still pushing Ghazala to marry the cousin with the land and the house and the military commission. I understood. It wasn't personal; her mother's obligation was to her daughter's well-being, not necessarily to her romantic happiness. What's the point of being in love with a penniless student if you're starving?

I turned down the row of bungalows. They were tidy and neat, with identical porches and small yards staked out by picket fencing.

Each step was a little heavier than the last.

Ghazala had confided to me how she'd stood up to her mother, an act of breathtaking courage. She had prayed for me to be president! My only asset was my education, my career — my *potential* career — as a lawyer. If I couldn't sit for the test, I might lose her forever. If I had to tell her I was too poor even to buy a chance at a respectable future, she would be heartbroken. Already, I could hear her mother hissing at her. *Didn't I tell you this guy is no good?* she'd say. *He can't even* take *his exams, let alone pass them*!

There was a wooden plaque screwed to each gate, on which the name and the title of the person living inside was painted in black. Six bungalows down the row, I found the one I was looking for: SHEIKH IMTIAZ, it said. PRINCIPAL OF THE LAW SCHOOL.

A car was parked inside the fence. He was probably home, instead of at a speaking engagement or delayed at the law school.

I took that as a small sign of divine intervention.

My heart thumped inside my chest, making a flat, repetitive thud in my ears. If the gate squeaked when I pushed it open, I didn't notice.

My finger, unnaturally light and almost numb, as if it were hollow, pushed a button next to the door. A bell rang. Footsteps padded toward the door. I took a deep breath, exhaled, rehearsed what I'd say.

Imtiaz opened the door. He was a tall man with fair skin and a squared-off mustache. He looked at me nonchalantly. "Yes?"

"Hello, sir," I said. "I'm sorry to disturb you, but my name is Muazzam . . . I mean, Khizr Khan." The words tumbled out, rapid with nerves. "I was in your evidence and criminal procedure class."

Imtiaz had been a prosecutor before he became a teacher, and he brought a wealth of anecdotes and real-life cases into his lectures. He was one of my favorite professors.

There was a flicker of recognition on Imtiaz's face. He nodded slowly. "Yes," he said again. "Well, what brings you here?"

"I'm supposed to take the exam tomorrow, but I have no money to pay the fee. I registered, and I thought I'd find the money but I haven't been able to, and, well, I didn't know where else to go."

He stared at me for a moment. "Are you prepared?"

"Yes, sir," I said. Then I blurted out my last gambit. "My life depends on taking this exam," I said. "Of course, I can take it next year, but that's next year."

Imtiaz stood there. I hadn't asked for anything, and wasn't sure what to ask for anyway. A waiver? Mercy? All I knew was that he was my last hope. I'd thrown myself into a void.

"Wait here," he said, and turned on his heel. From the porch, I watched him walk to a small writing desk. He pulled a sheet of paper from a drawer, wrote something on it with a pen, then folded the paper and sealed it in an envelope. He came back to the door and handed the envelope to me.

"Give this to the head proctor when you arrive," he said. "And get there early, in case arrangements have to be made."

I thanked him profusely, apologized again for interrupting his evening, and left. I closed the gate behind me and turned down the path toward the canal, staring at the envelope. I was overwhelmed with gratitude, but I didn't dare open it, though I longed to know what he had written. Surely he wouldn't have bothered to write a note that wouldn't be helpful?

Doubt crept into me, a shadow of the dusk beginning to settle over Lahore. What if it wasn't enough? What if he'd written, *Let this student take the exam when he can afford it?* Or, *Let him take the exam but hold his score until he can pay for it?* Neither of those would do me any good at all.

But why would he do that? Or, for that matter, why *wouldn't* he do that? He owed me nothing. Writing anything at all was merely a courtesy.

I was grateful and fearful all at once. It was a very long walk back to my dormitory.

I took the seven o'clock bus the next morning to Old Campus. The exam wasn't scheduled until nine, but I wasn't taking any chances. Students in the LL.B. program — it stands for the Latin for Bachelor of Laws — already were in the hallways, squatting on the floor and leaning against the walls, buried in books and leafing through notes, cramming a few precious last facts into their brain. I wasn't worried about studying — I'd been honest when I told my parents and Sheikh Imtiaz I was ready — only about whether I would be permitted to take the test.

The exam room was a large hall at the end

of the corridor, lined with desks bolted to the floor. A young man, an assistant proctor, stood like a sentry at the door.

"Do you have a roll number?" he asked.

"I'm not sure," I said. "Sheikh Imtiaz said I should give this to the head proctor." I held out my envelope, still not knowing what was written on the paper inside.

He looked at me skeptically but took the envelope, turned it over, studied it, looked at me again. He opened it, unfolded the note, read it, his glance alternating between the paper in his hands and the nervous student standing in front of him. "Wait," he said. He walked into the room, had a conversation with the proctor in charge of checking in students, showed him the note. There were some nods and casual shrugs, silent from my distance, before he came back.

"Okay, come on in," he said.

I sagged with relief. The proctor still held the note, and he turned it so I could read it. Imtiaz had written it on his official stationery, with his name and title embossed at the top. "Please allow this student to sit for the exam," it said. "It is my personal guarantee that his fees will be paid."

He'd signed it with his full name and printed his title below, as if to make certain no one would imagine I'd forged the note. I felt a hitch in my throat and a flush in my cheeks, a spasm of gratitude for such an act of faith and kindness. Imtiaz barely knew me, if he recognized me at all. He owed me nothing. Yet he had staked his reputation, and a sum of money, on me, merely because I had a need for which he was able to provide. I'd always been taught that people are fundamentally decent, and that each individual should be treated with as much dignity as I can muster. But to see it play out, to be the direct recipient of such kindness? To read Imtiaz's words?

Perhaps it seemed a minor gesture to him, a moment of jotting a few lines on a paper, nothing more. But the consequences for me were, literally, life-changing. Imtiaz was guaranteeing more than my fees. He was guaranteeing my chance at a future.

Lahore District Court was an ornate and compact red brick building on Lower Mall Road with a wide veranda behind four arches held up by eight white columns. It was set back from the street and surrounded by a thick green lawn and plots of flowers, a pretty and placid place after hours. When court was in session, though, it could be tense, the veranda crowded with plaintiffs and defendants and their lawyers, all those legal opponents jumbled together and waiting in the shade, trying to cool off before being called inside to one of the little courtrooms. Fistfights were not uncommon, as if a physical skirmish was just another part of the pretrial proceedings. Sometimes they were staged as diversions, allowing a handcuffed cousin to scoot off while the police guarding him dealt with his brawling family. Sometimes they were flat-out intimidation, as if to say *My witness is bigger than your witness.* And sometimes the heat and the stink and the anxiety combusted in tiny explosions.

The veranda was calm when we arrived. A little jostling was unavoidable, but there was no brawling. Maybe it was too early in the day. I carried a stack of files for civil cases: I'd begun my apprenticeship in the summer of 1973, after I'd taken my exam but before I'd gotten the results — I would find out later that I'd passed — and carrying files for a licensed veteran lawyer was one of my tasks. I'd shadow an attorney to court and watch how he performed in front of the judge. I learned how to draft briefs for civil cases and criminal continuances, and learned which forms had to be filed at which clerk's office. My sponsoring senior, an established and esteemed lawyer, taught me to read FIRs — First Investigative Reports, the initial write-ups police officers did of alleged crimes — as chronological narratives, to see the stories they told almost as movies, and then to pick out the incongruities, the spots where the continuity slipped. A criminal defense, my senior told me, was almost always hiding in those gaps.

Despite my ambivalence about actually practicing law, I was an eager apprentice, determined to draft the most precise briefs, to read every file front to back, to soak up as much tactical and technical knowledge as possible. That was my nature, fastidious and thorough.

The attorney I was shadowing that morning was an associate of my sponsoring senior. As we stood on the veranda together waiting for his case to be called, a man approached him, an ordinary-looking fellow, middle-aged with a beard, dressed in a business casual shirt and trousers. He was smiling, his hand extended. It was obvious that the attorney I was with knew him; he greeted him with joviality, then introduced me. The two of them chatted for a few moments. It was very professional, the two of them talking about clients and fees. "If you need me," the man said, "just call. You know where to find me." He shook the attorney's hand again and slipped into the crowd.

The attorney turned to me. "That," he said, "was a professional witness."

I was bemused. In the few weeks of my apprenticeship, I'd heard stories about professional witnesses, and I'd wanted to meet one. I'm not sure what I'd expected — a beady-eyed man slinking through the shadows, perhaps, his tongue split into a fork, a physical manifestation of his deformed morality. But he appeared to be a regular sort, not markedly different from anyone else milling outside the courthouse, except that he made his living arranging perjury.

A professional witness, I'd learned, was paid by lawyers to say whatever would be helpful in front of a judge. Need a fruit vendor to say your client was buying oranges at the time the murder was committed? That ordinary man could provide one. A truck driver to say he saw the robber racing away to the north, not the south where the defendant was arrested? A businessman to swear he was with your client when that widow sold him ten hectares for five hundred rupees? He could arrange those, too.

I was not taught about professional witnesses in law school, of course, other than obliquely in that perjury was a crime. Which meant professional witnesses were, by definition, criminals. Yet they also were a common and accepted adjunct to the Pakistani justice system.

Most lawyers in Pakistan are honest and honorable people. But law was not a codified system of rules that applied equally to everyone, but rather a malleable commodity, easily sabotaged by clerks who could make a file disappear and corrupt cops who could rewrite an FIR into implausible gibberish and witnesses who would testify to whatever truth was most lucrative.

I wasn't naïve. I had come of age under Ayub Khan, after all, had studied the radical poetry of Habib Jalib and Ahmad Faraz, had read the brave journalism of Shorish Kashmiri, who seemed to get himself arrested every few months. I knew Pakistani society functioned neither fairly nor humanely. Still, I was shocked by the depth and breadth of the corruption. We'd hear stories, sitting around the office, of families who'd bought their sons out of triple-homicide indictments. The most successful lawyers were those who, in the bland euphemism, "could get things done," which meant only that they knew how much to pay to what official. They were bagmen.

What was an honest lawyer to do? What was I to do, after I'd practiced for years for meager pay, after I'd built a reputation, a career, earned my way into the High Court cases for clients who could afford a reasonable fee? I didn't want to buy anyone out of anything. I would have to turn people away, let them find the lawyers who could get things done on their own. Yet that would make me complicit, a silent accomplice in a corrupt system.

The moral calculus was overwhelming. There had to be another option, but I had no idea what it was.

I'd gone to Sheikh Imtiaz not long after the exam to thank him for his generosity. Without his guarantee, I told him, I wouldn't have been able to sit for the test. But I still couldn't get my results, which had come in a few days earlier, and thus my license, without paying the fee.

"Of course," he said. "Do you think you'll be able to pay?"

"Yes, yes," I said quickly. I didn't have the money and didn't know how I'd get it, but I had my dignity.

"Are you sure? I can go ahead and pay it for you, for now."

"No," I said. "That won't be necessary.

You've done so much for me already."

I went back to my parents. I knew they would be expecting me. I'd told them about Sheikh Imtiaz, how he'd intervened, allowed me to sit for the exam.

My mother handed me a stack of rupees. "Your father has arranged it," she said.

I never knew how, exactly, but I assumed some was saved and some was borrowed. I clutched that stack tightly, as if the bills might float away or even disintegrate if I tried to count them. I slipped the money into my pocket, rode the bus back to Lahore, went straight to the university cashier, and laid all those bills delicately on the counter, still arranged into the same order in which my mother had given them to me.

The cashier wrote me a receipt, and I went across the hall to retrieve my results. I'd passed. Once I completed my apprenticeship, I would be a licensed attorney. I'd figure out the rest from there.

Ghazala's father had a bad heart, and his doctor, who was also one of his cousins, had his practice in Lahore. Her father traveled from Faisalabad with some regularity to see him. Near the end of 1973, he asked Ghazala to arrange a meeting with me the next time he was in Lahore.

Ghazala and I had known each other for eighteen months by then, and it was clear — to us, to our families — we wanted eventually to be married. But what *we* wanted was not of paramount importance. In our society, an engagement traditionally would be formalized between our families, my parents proposing to her parents, as marriage was considered far too serious for the bride and groom to agree upon on their own. My parents had, in fact, traveled to Faisalabad months earlier to begin those negotiations. We'd had a lively discussion before they left Gujranwala about whether they should bring sweets, a traditional gift of celebration; if a proposal was accepted, it would be rude not to have sweets at hand. My father, however, wisely counseled against it, because bringing pastries and candies was an all-or-nothing gamble. It would have put Ghazala's parents in the awkward position of either accepting or rejecting a gift and, thus, me. Better, he thought, to leave all options open, especially with Ghazala's mother pushing against her daughter's desire to commit herself to a lawyer destined to be, by her standards, impoverished and, possibly, beaten in the street by the police.

I met Ghazala's father after his appointment for tea in a tiny restaurant near Old Campus. He congratulated me on my exam and asked about my apprenticeship. I told him all was well, that I was learning a lot.

He was quiet for a moment, then spoke in a low, serious tone. "I admire you and what you're trying to do, Muazzam," he said.

He paused, staring into my eyes.

"You have my blessing," he said finally. "*Inshallah,* everything will go fine."

I had no sweets to give him, but the message was clear. *Inshallah,* Ghazala's mother would come around in time, would give her blessing, too.

"But promise me one thing," he said. "Promise me you will always take care of her. She is my dearest child. Promise me."

I felt the hitch in my throat again. For all my practicality, I've always been sentimental, too, my emotions quivering just below the surface, easily stirred. All grown up, and sunsets still made me melancholy. Now a man I admired, a good man, honest and kind and utterly devoted to his daughter, was entrusting her to me.

I took both his hands in mine. I blinked back grateful tears. "You need not worry," I said. "I will always take care of her."

He nodded, then pulled me into a strong hug. "I will pray for you," he whispered.

The professor who taught civil procedure was a very prominent man in Lahore, an attorney who eventually would be appointed a judge of the High Court, then the Supreme Court. Because of his connections and his generally affable manner, he was quite popular among the students, always drawing a cluster of us when he appeared on campus outside the classroom.

One morning in early 1974 when I happened to be in the law college, the professor parked his car and came inside at the far end of the long hallway that ran the length of the ground floor. Almost immediately, half a dozen students, including me, surrounded him. He was in a typically gregarious mood.

"You've done well on your exams, yes?" he asked. "Everyone's apprenticeship going well?"

We all nodded enthusiastically.

He brightened, as if he'd just remembered something important. "I've just heard of a company in Dubai that's looking to hire people," he said. "People with a legal background, preferably. If any of you are interested, come and see me."

We nodded more enthusiastically.

The professor started to turn away, then stopped and patted the sides of his coat, feeling for a slight lump in one of the pockets. He grinned, pulled out a sheet of paper, unfolded it. "Wait," he said, "I have it right here. Send a résumé and a letter if you want to go to Dubai."

He held out the paper and I scribbled down the name of the company, Robray Offshore Drilling, and the address, a post office box in Dubai.

A decade earlier, Dubai had survived as a trading post at the mouth of the Persian Gulf. Then oil was discovered offshore in 1966. Exports began three years later, and two more offshore fields were being explored by 1973. The emirate was in the midst of an oil boom that would bring the enormous wealth Dubai is known for today. Robray was one of the companies rushing in to make its fortune.

Not that I knew any of that then. I knew nothing about the oil business, either, but that didn't matter. Robray was looking for office staff, which was all I needed to know. I had a college degree and in a few months would have a professional license. Surely I could cope with whatever administrative tasks needed attending. The pay wasn't specified, just "appropriate remuneration," but I assumed that a foreign oil-services company in Dubai would pay more than what a newly minted lawyer could earn in Pakistan. That was my only concern, immediate and practical: to make enough money to properly support Ghazala and, ideally, start saving for a bar-at-law degree in England. My law license was fine, but it wasn't enough; now I had to study English law, learn more, open myself as a vessel for knowledge. I did not yet feel complete. Marrying Ghazala would get me most of the way there, but I still had more to learn.

I typed my résumé and composed a letter in English, carefully editing and proofreading to make certain my punctuation marks were in their correct positions and my grammar was impeccable. My grandfather's lessons so long before — *Eat. Go.* — had been immensely helpful. I sealed it in an envelope, affixed the postage, and sent it to the post office box in Dubai.

The reply came at the very end of winter, not long before I formally received my law license in April. I'd been hired. There was an employment contract in the envelope that said the pay was fifteen hundred dirhams a month. I calculated the exchange rate quickly in my head — that was thirty-seven hundred and fifty rupees, almost three times what I could expect to make in Pakistan for the foreseeable future. It wasn't outlandish wealth by any means, the equivalent of about $1,900 today, but to me it was an extraordinary salary.

I took a bus to Faisalabad to tell Ghazala. This was what I'd been hoping for, an opportunity to prove myself, a chance to circumvent the early, punishing years of a legal career in Pakistan. True, I would be leaving the country before we were married — her father's blessing went only so far; we still needed her mother's — but that seemed a worthy sacrifice, more of an investment in our future.

But what if Ghazala was opposed? She had gotten her master's degree in Persian and had a good job teaching at the women's college in Faisalabad. What if she wanted to remain in Pakistan, build a career, weather the Bhutto years, chaotic yet promising to me, a destructive repudiation of Ayub Khan to her? Our political differences had never been more than a topic of light conversation — neither of us was strident or prone to polemics, and Pakistan was in such disarray that we would have been squabbling only over degrees of chaos. But what if she asked me to stay? What if she wanted me to start practicing law right away, establish myself in a profession I wasn't sure I wanted to be a part of in a country where I wasn't sure I wanted to live?

That would be a difficult conversation.

"Ghazala, I've been offered a job," I told her over tea in her family's living room. "The money is very good, enough that we could get married and I could still save for school overseas. It's a law job, too." I front-loaded all of the positive details, racing through them. Her eyes brightened, and a smile spread over her face.

"But it's in Dubai," I said.

Her smile didn't waver. "Really? That's wonderful," she said.

"Do you think I should take it?"

"What? Of course you should take it!"

"Will you come later?"

"Yes," she said. "Yes. You know I will come."

My head was spinning with relief. There would be no difficult conversation. Somehow, against all probability, everything seemed to be working out. I'd been able to take my exam, passed it, found a way out of Pakistan, and managed to keep Ghazala, too. My fortunes had changed immeasurably in less than a year, and my future appeared brilliant, shining just over the horizon.

A one-way ticket to Dubai cost money that I, once again, didn't have. But I was less ashamed asking my parents this time, even though I knew they would have to borrow from someone, as I had a job now, a plan, a future. I would be able to pay them back for the ticket, for the exam fees, for everything. The tea seller would finally get paid for all those egg sandwiches, and my cafeteria tab would be squared. In a few months, maybe a year, Ghazala's mother would see that I was worthy and capable and deeply loved her daughter. She would give her blessing, Ghazala and I would marry, and Ghazala would come to live as my wife in Dubai. Already her mother was warming to me as a prospective husband: She came with Ghazala to see me off at the airport, which I considered a very good sign.

I was leaving everything I'd ever known. My world did not yet extend beyond Gujranwala and Lahore and Faisalabad. I was twenty-four years old and I'd never flown on an airplane, never seen the ocean, let alone crossed one. England was a place professors returned from, and America was no more than a chimera I'd read about two years before. I knew it was out there, this political ideal, but to me a way of thinking and governing and living more than a physical place. Every so often, something — a seized press, a beaten Black Coat — would nudge a memory of sitting in my dorm, studying an almost mystical document. But I'd had to put political theory aside while I got on with the rest of my life.

Yet I was not afraid. It required only a subtle shift in perspective to ease any anxiety. I wasn't leaving so much as I was going forward. To what, I wasn't entirely sure, only that there was hope in the future. *Tomorrow will be better,* I told myself, over and over, until tomorrow became everything to me. That hope became so enormous that it was all I thought of. In it, I saw all the promise of everything that was possible.

CHAPTER 4
TOMORROW WILL BE BETTER

The plane landed in Dubai late on a Friday afternoon, taxied down a runway paved into the desert, and pulled up to a small terminal. The big waves of foreign workers were only beginning to arrive in the emirate, and there was no tourist trade to speak of, so there was no need yet for the enormous airport with three terminals that now sprawls across more than seven thousand acres. In the spring of 1974, there were only four gates, and even that seemed ambitious.

An immigration officer stamped my visa, and I continued into the arrival hall. It was crowded with locals picking up relatives and friends, but there was no one waiting for me. Maybe I should have been intimidated, traveling overseas for the first time, alone. But I wasn't. I was determined, focused. One could make the case, I suppose, that I was determined and focused *because* I was intimidated, but that assumes a level of introspection I was aware of neither then nor now. I wasn't in a foreign country so much as I was in the place that was providing me gainful employment and a chance at a better life. That shifts your perspective quite effectively.

I didn't start work until Monday and had nowhere to go before then. I loitered outside near a line of mismatched Datsuns and Toyotas, each a different color, with TAXI painted on the side. The crowd gradually thinned until it disappeared completely, and it was only me and the taxis.

I saw a driver standing near one of the cars dressed in *shalwar kameez.* He was young and not very tall, but I could tell by his clothing he was Pakistani. At the very least, he would speak Urdu. I approached him.

"Are you from Pakistan?" I asked.

"Yes."

"I've just come in and my job starts on Monday," I said. "I need a place to stay."

He cocked an eyebrow, shook his head. "I don't know of anyplace," he said. "There are very few hotels and they are all very expensive."

I was not prepared for that. I'd left Pakistan with only a few rupees in my pocket, which I'd converted to dirhams in the airport, enough, I'd thought, for a few plain meals and a modest guesthouse room. But apparently there were no rooms that could accommodate my budget. Demand for housing in Dubai far outstripped supply. People were paying the equivalent of hundreds of dollars in today's money for plank walls covered with a tarp and perched on the roof of another building.

The cabbie considered my situation for a moment. "I think, he said, "that you are welcome to stay with me."

I was happily surprised but not startled by his generosity. The cabbie clearly wasn't a wealthy man, but he was offering the only thing he had: shelter. It did not occur to me to be wary, that perhaps he was a criminal who'd found a target. His clean clothes suggested he'd been to Friday prayers, and even a casual Muslim understands the teaching to care for the stranger as your own brethren. "Yes, thank you," I said. "Thank you."

I put my one brown suitcase in the trunk and climbed into the back seat. The taxi drove off into an old part of Dubai, narrow streets cluttered with shanties and low shops on the north side of the creek dredged a decade earlier to handle heavier shipping traffic. The cabbie steered down one tight lane, then another, into a warren of low buildings of mud bricks and cinder blocks. He stopped in front of one that was not noticeably different from the others, a beige lump that seemed to have been pushed up from the sand into three rooms and a roof.

I asked how much the rent would be.

"Don't worry about the rent," he said, waving me off.

I gave him a few bills for the fare and followed him inside. There was a kitchen with a burner for the teakettle, a toilet off to one side, and two bare rooms. The cabbie scuttled into the one where his brother slept and gathered up the few items inside — a thin mattress, some clothes — and left it completely empty except for a naked bulb hanging from a cord in the center of the ceiling. It was square and small, no more than ten feet by ten feet, with a concrete floor, block walls, and no window.

The brother was out, but he would share the other room with the cabbie, who went back to work. I was left alone in their home.

There was no bed in the room, but at least I wasn't on the street. I opened my suitcase, fished out my towel, and spread it on the floor for a mattress. I changed out of my traveling outfit into more comfortable *shalwar kameez,* then shook out my other clothes to use as a blanket. Finally, I closed the suitcase; that would be my pillow.

I shut the door and lay down. I was hoping the cabbie — I'd not gotten his name — would be home soon. I was hungry and wanted to know where I could get something to eat. But I fell asleep. When I awoke, it was very late, too late to be disturbing anyone.

I stayed there, supine in my dark cube, the gift of a stranger, and prayed that tomorrow would be a better day.

There was a Lebanese bakery not far from the cabdriver's house, and I walked there in the morning through dusty streets that had no names, the Dubai heat already rising under the Arabian sun. Other people already were out, an eclectic mix of locals and workers imported from India, Bangladesh, Lebanon, Africa. I didn't feel out of place, because no one seemed to really have a claim to the place.

At the bakery, bread sprinkled with spices and herbs and a cup of tea cost one dirham. I could afford that. It was a modest meal, eaten while standing against a wall outside, but when your stomach is empty and you're far from home, the simplest food can be a marvelous feast. I felt immediately and immensely better. While I ate, I did the math in my head. One dirham was equal to three rupees, and tea and bread in Lahore could be bought for thirty paisas (a paisa being worth one hundredth of a rupee) — which meant that the price in Dubai was ten times higher. My promised salary had seemed like a fortune to me, but I realized I would need to be frugal nonetheless.

I'd arrived two days early on purpose, to give myself time to acclimate, find a place to live, learn my way around. Since I had a roof over me, at least for the next two nights, all that was left was to explore the city. I meandered through the old neighborhoods for a while, then crossed the creek that bisected the emirate into what was becoming the new Dubai. The buildings were bigger there, five and six stories, and construction cranes rose like a scattered steel forest against the deep blue of the sky. The billionaires' playground that Dubai would become was years away, but it was obvious even then that the emirate was making a frantic leap forward. The creek was like a wide line separating the past from the future, both a metaphor and a physical boundary. I couldn't help but see it as a metaphor for my own life, too, the foreigner squatting in a stranger's house on the old side who would cross the canal on Monday to the new side, to a job and a paycheck, to a new and richer life.

The office of Robray Offshore Drilling was in a newer building about midway between the canal and the gulf, six stories of drab cement block with balconies jutting out from the upper floors. It was nothing special to look at, but I'd know where I was walking come Monday morning.

By the time I'd found the building, the sun was midway across the sky, bright and blazing. I'd accomplished my only real task in half a day, and I had an entire afternoon and one more full day to fill. There was nothing else to do but walk. I wandered back to the creek and followed it to the beach. The gulf sparkled in front of me, sunlight catching the wavelets, tiny flashes and pops of white all the way to the horizon. The sparkling pale sand beach stretched to the south, and children splashed in the surf. The view must have been breathtaking, especially for a young man who'd never seen so much water, but I barely noticed. I was lost in anxious thought.

When would I get paid? I couldn't squat in the cabbie's brother's room indefinitely — where would I live, and how could I afford it? Tea and bread ten times the price at home! I was supposed to be an earner for the family. I had debts to pay. And Ghazala — I already missed her terribly and longed to have her with me. But first I needed money. I supposed all of the dreamers in the world must face this moment, when the future butts up against the immediate present. Fantasies are deferred, must be deferred, because first there is the necessity of work.

I walked for hours, down the beach and back again, along the creek, tracing a lazy route back to Old Dubai and a stranger's spare room. The day dragged on forever. But that, I decided, was how many of my days would seem; there is sometimes a staggering distance between what one wants and how one will achieve it. But I maintained — always maintained — my hope, which I was sure was more confidence than delusion. I slowly fell into a fitful sleep, telling myself the same thing I'd said before I left Pakistan: Tomorrow will come, surely as the sun will rise, and tomorrow will be better.

Tomorrow was not better. I had nothing to do on Sunday but wait for Monday, so I walked again. I wandered the narrow streets of the old city in the morning, crossed the creek and followed it to the beach in the early afternoon, meandered for hours, going everywhere and nowhere.

Too much empty time can be a curse. When there is nothing immediate for the mind to focus on, it can drift to the abstract and the existential, to what might happen and what might not. It will seize on uncertainty, massage doubts into fears, anxiety into dread. On Saturday, the newness of the city and the task of finding my way around had ameliorated my worries, tamped them down into manageable concerns. But on the second day, Dubai was already becoming familiar. There was nothing to distract me.

I calculated numbers in my head, exchange rates and housing costs and the price of food. My salary no longer seemed extraordinary. Where would I live? Could I even afford a cement hovel like the cabbie's? How could I pay my debts, let alone save anything?

Dusk was settling over the old city. I turned a corner near the bakery where bread was ten times the price in Lahore. My stomach burbled. I'd been walking all day in the sun, but hadn't eaten anything since Saturday morning.

I fingered the few bills in my pocket, counted them without pulling them out.

How long would they have to last before I got paid? A week? Two? I could afford a meager meal of bread and tea, I thought. But then: No, I couldn't. What would I eat tomorrow or the next day? What if I needed to pay for a room? I would insist on paying the cabbie, though I suspected he would decline. But what if he didn't?

My gut twitched, as if it was grasping for any undigested bits that might be lingering inside me.

There was a garbage bin against the wall. On top there was a package of bread, opened and almost empty, but two tandoori loaves were still tucked inside.

I glanced around furtively, like a nervous thief. No one was paying attention to me.

I sidled up to the trash can as casually as possible, snapped my hand out, grabbed the bag, and curled it under my arm in one motion so smooth and deft that I told myself no one had noticed. My stride quickened, and my eyes stared at the dusty ground.

My cheeks burned.

I was ashamed.

At the cabbie's house, I inspected my dinner. The loaves were stale, hard and dry, but clean. I ate them with a glass of water. *Look at you,* I thought as I chewed. *Look how far you've come — all the way to Dubai to eat a pauper's meal.*

The bread filled my stomach, a wet lump of chewed-up dough that would hold me until morning. Until tomorrow. Maybe, I told myself, the next tomorrow really will be better.

The elevator doors slid apart on the fourth floor, opening onto a small corridor and, directly across, a solid door with the words ROBRAY OFFSHORE DRILLING stenciled at eye level and flanked by glass sidelights. I peeked through one and glanced around quickly. An Indian woman sat behind a desk with a telephone and a typewriter, a credenza set perpendicularly off the corner so that the furniture formed an L. A handful of men, a mix of Pakistanis and local Arabs by the looks of them, waited in a line. Applying for jobs, I guessed. And the entire floor, I noticed, was covered in carpet. I had been in nice offices in Pakistan, those of professors and prominent attorneys, and they often had beautiful rugs, but never anything so extravagant that it stretched from wall to wall. Eventually, I'd come to know that it was nothing special, just a commercial-grade beige weave, but at that moment I'd never seen anything so luxurious.

I tapped on the door and opened it without waiting for a reply. The Indian woman looked up, and I introduced myself. Her name was Margaret Pinto; I'd soon come to learn she had been the first person hired by Robray in Dubai. She was the secretary, office manager, kitchen organizer, translator, and occasional fetcher of doughnuts from the bakery a few buildings down the road.

"My name is Khizr Khan," I said by way of introduction. No one in Dubai would be calling me by the familiar, affectionate Muazzam. "I've been hired, and I'm here to see Mr. Crowell."

"Oh, yes," Margaret said. She smiled, and seemed genuinely happy to see me, a new colleague in an understaffed office. She offered me a chair and, after a few minutes, ushered me into Allen Crowell's office.

Allen was the operations manager, an oilman for many decades, and the first American I'd ever met. He was in his early fifties, tall and white-haired with blue eyes, a sharp nose, and big hands, which I couldn't help but notice when he gripped mine. He greeted me enthusiastically, as if he, too, was delighted that help had finally arrived. And then he immediately got down to business.

"We're hiring a lot of people," he said,

"and we've got two months to get staffed up. Your job is to get everyone processed and the paperwork organized." He pointed at three piles on his desk. "We're hiring locals for the warehouse, materials guys, drivers, laborers. We've got roughnecks and roustabouts coming in from Houston, and their visas all need to be straightened out . . ."

I was already getting confused. Paperwork I could handle. But I had no idea what a roughneck or a materials man was. Allen kept talking, explaining basic procedures I could understand yet sprinkled with titles and terms so unfamiliar he might as well have been speaking fragments of Mandarin.

". . . and your office is the one right over here." Allen was leading me out the door and a few steps across the reception area. "You can set it up any way you want," he said, "however you think it's going to work best for you. But, like I said, we've only got two months —"

Allen stopped abruptly. He was looking at me with mild concern.

"Where are you staying?" he asked.

I told him a cabdriver had put me up for a few nights and that I was still looking for a permanent place. I didn't tell him I was sleeping on a towel on the floor with a suitcase for a pillow, or that my only shower since leaving Pakistan had required boiling water on a small burner and then draining it through a bucket. But I must have looked exhausted.

I was still talking, saying I'd look for a room to rent soon, when Allen picked up the phone on my new desk. "Yeah, we need to get him a place," I heard him say. "No, right now." It was a very brief conversation. He hung up and led me back to his office.

Allen spent the next half hour explaining my job. He showed me employment contracts and immigration forms and copies of visas. From my lazy strolls around Dubai, I'd suddenly accelerated into a frenetic start-up operation. What wasn't already moving at a breakneck pace would soon have to be. I would have to make sure everything was filled out properly and approved by the local authorities, whom I didn't know yet, and ferry copies from our office to the airport. I'd been hoping my law license would be required, or at least useful. It wasn't: My job, it appeared, was glorified clerical work. But Allen did give me the title of legal director.

A woman came in, white, about Allen's age, slender, with blond hair and dark green eyes. She was very pretty, and she carried herself with a natural elegance. Allen introduced her as his wife, Lisa. "Okay, let's go to your home," she said. She had a German accent. Allen had worked all over the world and had met her in Germany. "Do you have things you need to get?"

I thought for a moment that I'd misheard. My home? I didn't have a home. Surely she didn't mean the cabbie's squat rooms. Why would she want to see those? The gears in my head clicked a few turns, put Lisa's words into the correct context: She and Allen were providing me with a home. I was stunned.

"Yes," I stammered. "Yes, only a few things."

Allen drove me over the creek. The street where the cabbie lived was too narrow for Allen's station wagon to fit, so he parked as close as he could and waited while I retrieved my suitcase. I looked around my borrowed room, so bare and modest. Yet where would I have gone without the kindness of a stranger? How much more bedraggled would I be without my friend the cabbie?

I could see a bemused grin on Allen's face as I walked back. "Is that it?" he said.

I told him it was. He let out a quick, soft chuckle. It struck me as affectionate rather than condescending.

We drove back across the canal, made a few turns, and stopped in front of a plain block building six or seven stories tall. There were boxes in the back of the station wagon, and Lisa distributed them among us, two to me, a heavy one to Allen, one for herself. I followed them into the elevator, balancing my boxes. We got off on the fifth floor and went a short way down the hall, where Allen unlocked the door to a one-bedroom apartment.

The drilling platforms were so far offshore that the men worked in two-week shifts, two on and two off. When they were on land, they needed a place to live. If they had families with them, and many of them did, their wives and children needed a permanent home. So Robray, as well as the other companies operating in Dubai, leased as many apartments as they could, bidding against one another for scarce properties, driving up rents. They were set aside for senior expats, to which the legal director from Pakistan apparently had been promoted.

"This is where you'll stay," Allen said. I knew instinctively he wasn't going to charge me — Allen knew how much I was paid, and he knew this place cost more than that.

It wasn't a fancy apartment, but to me, especially after sleeping on a concrete floor, it was paradise. There were windows in the bedroom and living room overlooking the street and letting in the late morning light. There were three pillows on the bed, more than I'd ever slept with, and a tub in the bathroom, which I'd never had before, either.

Lisa started unpacking boxes. She'd brought everything I would need to settle in. Towels and cooking pans and forks and spoons. There was already tea in the cupboard and a kettle on the counter, and the refrigerator was filled with basic foodstuffs, eggs and milk and bread and butter and jam.

Something, I thought, must have happened overnight. I couldn't believe my good fortune, that I was deserving of so much. Tomorrow really was better than yesterday.

"Take the rest of the day off, get some rest," Allen told me. "You'll start tomorrow." I walked him to the door, and he gave me a hundred-dirham bill. "In case you need anything," he said.

I closed the door, looked around my new home. And then I cried, waves of emotion pouring out of me. I was humbled and grateful and exhausted all at once, overwhelmed by the generosity of Lisa and Allen. Were all Americans like this? Is this what that country, with its freedoms wrought from rebellion, produced? Did a nation of laws, of equal dignity for all, instill in its people a basic goodness?

I had met only one American. A minuscule sample size for a rigorous demographic survey. But the early results were promising.

When I'd regained my composure, I realized I was hungry. I made a cup of tea, spread butter and jam on toast, and sat at the table in the kitchen. *My* kitchen. It was heavenly.

My clothes were clean and ironed and I was rested and well fed when I went to work Tuesday morning. I figured out the routines of my job pretty quickly, and fell into an easy rhythm of gathering paperwork and sorting files.

I had four filing cabinets in my office. Two were for the local hires, mostly laborers and warehouse workers and the like. There was a constant stream of men coming into the office to apply, so many that Allen soon switched offices with me. His had been the first one inside the door, across from Margaret Pinto, and the steady shuffling of feet on the carpet past his door was distracting. Better to put me up front.

The people looking for work almost always had a sad story to tell — perhaps a boss who wasn't paying them, or at least not enough to survive. I always believed them, and felt a pang of sympathy. I thought of the taxi driver who'd given me shelter, driving people around Dubai for three years and all he could afford were two cement-floored and windowless rooms he had to share with his brother. But there was nothing I could do beyond empathize and try not to make the applicants' lives any more difficult. I would take down their information, would make sure that their applications were filled out correctly and, if they were foreigners, that their residency papers were in order and filed away in my cabinets.

The other two cabinets were for the expats. Robray hired people from all over the world for the rig jobs. There were Australians and Brits and, mostly, Americans, but they all were initially processed through an office in Houston. Every morning, I'd come in to find a roll of paper unspooled from the fax machine, loose curls of employment contracts and photocopied travel documents tumbling across my credenza.

Over the first few weeks, I developed a

system to deal with the Dubai bureaucracy, which was neither modern nor efficient. I would have Houston fax me a new hire's employment contract and a copy of the first page of his passport. Usually, the passport information was written on a separate sheet. But mistakes happened, and if just one number or a middle initial was off, a visa could be held in emirate purgatory until it got straightened out; it was better for me to have an actual copy to work from. I would take those documents to the immigration office, where I became such a familiar face that the officers barely looked up from their tea as they stamped my pile of entry visas. The visas then had to be delivered to the airport, but I was always careful to stop at the office first and make a backup copy for my files. It wasn't unheard-of for visas to be misplaced, stall a new hire coming into the emirate and strand him at the airport overnight and most of the following day. That's why I carried the copy with me when I went to pick people up.

The flights usually landed in the hours after midnight, KLM and Lufthansa and Singapore Airlines planes setting down in the desert dark. One of the customs officers would holler when one of our hires arrived — "Robray! Robray!" — but they weren't difficult to spot. Most of them were a little drunk, and a few of them were a lot drunk, drinking being their preferred way to pass the time in airports and on airplanes. But they were a generally affable lot. The Brits and Australians and assorted Europeans were always polite, if somewhat reserved. The Americans quickly became my favorites. They were the friendliest, the most genuine, the ones who'd stick out a big, weathered hand and say, "Hi, I'm Jim." They never expected to be called "Mister," never asked anyone to carry their bags. They came from Abilene, Amarillo, or Richardson, Texas, an assortment of little cities and small towns I'd never heard of but that I imagined probably had a lot of people riding around on horseback. And in the morning, they would come to my office and always, without fail, ask for a beer permit. They'd been told when they were hired that they wouldn't be able to buy alcohol in a Muslim emirate without a permit, and they didn't waste any time getting one. I found that completely charming, how upfront and blunt they were. They never asked for a *liquor* permit the way the Brits and Australians did, and then only after a day or two, as if it were a casual afterthought that they might want to mix a proper gin and tonic or sip a cordial. The Americans only wanted cold beer, and as soon as possible. I'd reach for one of the permits the police had given us, each already stamped with the company logo and a blank line for me to fill in a name and a title. I always did so with a knowing smile. In Dubai, it was 115 degrees in the shade. It seemed perfectly reasonable for a cowboy to want a cold beer.

A few days after I started, Allen came into my office clutching a stack of six U.S. passports. They belonged to the wife and children of a man named Will Wilkerson, who strode in right behind him. Will was a tall, white-haired American with what I'd come to recognize as a Louisiana twang. He had a pronounced limp, two mangled fingers on his left hand, and a face lined and chapped by years of the sun and salt air that swirled around the offshore rigs. "You're not as safe out there as you are in the office," he told me once I got to know him better, referring to the limp and the fingers.

Will was Robray's drilling superintendent, one of the company's most senior positions. I liked him right away. He always wore coveralls and he never came to the office empty-handed; he usually brought doughnuts, not the cake ones but the light, yeasty kind with a light glaze, from the same Lebanese bakery Margaret went to. I'd never had doughnuts in Pakistan.

"Will needs some help with immigration," Allen told me, holding out the pile of passports. Most of the senior expats brought their families over, but none of the others had five children. The Dubai authorities wanted to see him in the flesh, make sure he was a real person with real relatives, not a phantom trying to sneak people into the country. Will could pull crude from miles beneath the seabed, but he needed me to guide him through the creaky Dubai bureaucracy.

"Sure," I said, "I can arrange that." In the bubble and churn of Dubai, no one thought it odd that immigration was handled by an immigrant, though, really, who better to have figured out the system? I'd made friends quickly with the men in the immigration office. "But maybe you should wear a jacket," I told Will. Official business went more smoothly in proper attire.

Will grinned at that. "You got it," he said.

He returned a week or so later, wearing slacks and a jacket, the only time I would ever see him not in coveralls.

"I'm parked down front," Will said. "We can take my car."

We took the elevator down and walked out into the late-morning heat. I slid into the passenger seat of Will's brown Impala, he turned the key, and that big American engine rumbled. He pushed a plastic box into the center of the dashboard. I'd never seen an eight-track tape before. There was a soft click, and then music started to play. Will reached for a knob to turn the volume down.

"Wait," I said.

The sticker on the edge said RAY PRICE. There was steady rhythm, a 4/4 beat, unfamiliar but completely natural. I could understand the words, and they were telling a story.

"What is that?"

Will cocked an eyebrow at me. "Really?" He smiled. "That's country music."

He reached for the knob again, as if I'd heard enough.

"No, don't," I said. "Let it play."

We listened to Ray Price all the way to the immigration office and all the way back. I borrowed tapes from Will for months after that — Conway Twitty and Kenny Rogers and the great Johnny Cash — and listened to them over and over, the eight-tracks clicking through their cycles. I loved it, this country music. So different from what I'd listened to in Pakistan, almost as if the notes and chords were transmissions from an alien world, wonderful and harmonious and brimming with stories to tell.

Ghazala's father died on May 30, 1974. A heart attack, his third.

She was devastated. She adored her father almost as much as he adored her, if that was possible. I was crushed, too. Her father was an honorable man, benevolent and noble, when he had so many opportunities to be neither. His integrity struck me as virtue nearing holiness. He was also my ally. He believed in me, in my love for his daughter.

Ghazala called me as soon as she could, dialing from a telephone exchange in Faisalabad, one of our few phone calls. I contacted my parents immediately after, but they already knew; one of Ghazala's relatives had made the trip to Gujranwala to tell them. I asked them to go to Faisalabad as soon as possible to offer their condolences. This was critical, a sign of respect and affection and shared grief, one family to another with which they hoped to combine. It didn't matter that sweets had never been presented to honor our engagement: My love for Ghazala and my family's affection for her required they go at once to Fai-salabad.

It pained me terribly that I could not be there as well.

Death, or the grief that follows, has a disturbing tendency to sharpen one's focus, to filter out the chaff and the extraneous distractions. For me, of course, I developed tunnel vision on Ghazala, on the future I desperately hoped we would have together.

I knew even then that Dubai was only temporary. All things considered, I had a good job at Robray. But I wasn't planning on making a career of it. From almost the moment the jet's wheels had touched down, I had been thinking ahead, calculating how long it would be before I could leave.

I had everything plotted out, if not on a precise timeline, at least in a proper order. I got myself settled, started collecting my paychecks. With money coming in, I'd begun paying off all my debts — to my parents, the tea seller, the cafeteria — and sent home a little extra when I could. Whatever was left after feeding myself, I saved. I needed to convince Ghazala's parents that I could take care of her, that I had the funds to provide a good life. I hated the distance between us. When people say they will write every day, they don't often mean it literally (or, if they do, the letters get quite tedious very quickly), but we wrote each other as often as we could. She had finished her degree and returned to Faisalabad, where she was thrilled to be a professor of Persian at the women's college from which she herself had graduated a few years earlier. But I wanted her with me, in Dubai or anywhere else, as my partner and companion.

I continued to think, too, about my own education. I needed to save for that as well, enough to get myself and the family I hoped we would have to England or the United States. I'd always assumed I would go to London, because that is where most of the people I knew of with advanced degrees had studied; the gravity of the colonial past still contained Pakistan in an Anglo orbit. I would study the law again, layering more expertise on top of my Pakistani license, perhaps parlay that into teaching or, at the very least, use it to leapfrog up the professional order.

My plans were not a secret. I'd gotten to be friends with Allen and Lisa and had told them of my ambitions. They often invited me over for dinner, and if there were other guests or if their grown-up children were

143

visiting, Allen would sometimes introduce me as "Khizr, a lawyer who's saving money to go back to school."

That wasn't going to happen soon. That much I understood. But I could be patient. In the meantime, I was good at what I did.

A few months into my job, Allen decided I was spending too much on taxis ferrying me to the immigration office and the airport and back again. "We need to get you a car," he told me.

I wasn't opposed to the idea. But there were two problems. One was that I didn't have a license, and getting one required passing a test. I'd never driven before, let alone parallel parked, which was the part of the exam everyone told me was the most difficult. Allen let me practice in his big Chevy wagon, puttering around the parking lot and maneuvering between a pair of cones set on the pavement. I'd back up, turn the wheel, pull forward, turn it again, reverse, three times, six, twelve, until I'd wedged his car into a vaguely straight position. I kept at it, pretend-parking over and over, gradually reducing the number of times I'd have to go back and forth to a respectable three. It wasn't perfect parking, but it was reasonably competent.

When I went to the motor vehicle office, I

caught a break: The officer administering it put me behind the wheel of a Datsun sedan, maybe half the size of Allen's Chevy. I followed all of his directions — turn right here, left there, pull over — and did fine. Then he told me to park parallel to the curb. I gripped the steering wheel a little tighter to squeeze the tremble out of my hands, shifted into reverse, and nudged the gas pedal. The rear wheels slid next to the curb but didn't touch it. I braked, turned the wheel, pulled forward, put the car into park. The Datsun had been much easier to handle than the station wagon, the margin of error several feet wider. It was a bit askew, the front a foot or so closer to the curb than the rear, but it was good enough. I passed.

I proudly showed my new license to Allen, quite pleased with myself. "All right," Allen said. "Good for you. Now we have to get you a car."

That led to the second problem. I couldn't afford a car. I was barely putting aside enough as it was. But I didn't protest. I knew Allen was right, and I assumed we'd work something out. Still, I looked for the cheapest vehicle I could find, paging through the stapled pages of a used-car magazine until I saw a little white Toyota. The couple selling it were asking four thousand dirhams, almost three months' pay.

Allen made the phone call, arranged for the sellers to come to the office. He looked it over, poking around under the hood and pushing down on the fenders to check the suspension. He seemed satisfied, and I was grateful for his help; all I knew about cars was where the steering wheel and the pedals were supposed to be, and they seemed to be in their proper positions. Allen did the negotiating, too: If we bought it on the spot, we could have the Toyota for only three thousand.

"Do you like it?" he asked me.

"Yes, yes," I said. What else could I say?

"All right then." Allen pulled out a checkbook, paid the couple, signed all the papers, then drove them home in his Chevy. I had a car.

"I know you need your money right now," Allen told me when he got back to the office. "So don't worry about it. But maybe later, when you get a bonus, you can pay some of it back. Good?"

Yes, of course that was good. I was relieved — Allen could have just made the check a straight advance on my salary — and overwhelmed by his generosity. Again.

Allen and Lisa became America to me. I

had a memory of the Declaration from my law school class, but that hadn't ignited a passionate study of the United States, hadn't stirred a desire even to visit. The truth is, it was easy to forget those moments of intellectual wonder in the daily grind of trying to lift myself toward my future. But these two people took me in, embraced me. Even today, I can feel how genuinely kind and caring both were to me. They didn't owe me anything. They were warm and generous out of the goodness of their hearts, for no other reason. When I reflect now, as I often do, about how humbly grateful I am for all that America has given me, I know that my gratitude begins with them, with those early days in Dubai. They had done enough in hiring me. Allen could have just paid my wages and let me fend for myself. Instead, they looked after me. They sheltered me in more comfort than I'd ever known. They invited me into their own home, where Lisa cooked turkey and steak, wonderful foods I'd never tasted. Allen bought me a car. They were my friends. My American friends.

We always worked late at Robray, well into the evening. Allen left that night shortly after seven o'clock. "Drive carefully now, Khizr," he called over his shoulder. "You've

147

got your very own car now, so I won't have to worry about you."

I fingered the key in my pocket. I stayed in the office for another hour, organizing files, finishing paperwork, working quickly. When I finally left, my heart beat a little faster, and my cheeks flushed with a tingle of excitement. I stared at the Toyota, walked around it, marveled at it. My first car. I got in, turned the key, then sat listening to the engine, inspecting the interior. There was the radio, and here was the fan, and this lever made the wipers flap back and forth, and that lever made the turn signals blink. An old, used sedan can seem so precious from the right perspective.

How I wished Ghazala were sitting in the passenger seat, taking it all in with me, popping open the glove box, fiddling with the tuner. I drove very slowly to my apartment, and I parked in an isolated spot, far away from other cars, so that mine wouldn't get scraped or dinged. I wanted Ghazala to see it for the first time just as I had, and I wasn't sure when that would be.

After Ghazala's father died, her mother finally agreed that we could marry. I was proving myself in Dubai, working as a professional with a respectable salary. The

148

cost of living meant I wasn't as well off as perhaps another potential husband would be, but my future was promising and my present wasn't too bad, either. I had promised her father I would always take care of Ghazala, and her mother now believed I was capable of it. And she was a widow now — it was time for a husband to provide for her daughter.

I saved as much of my paycheck as I could, and by the late autumn of 1974, I'd set aside enough to bring Ghazala to Dubai and begin our life together. I'd saved enough, in fact, to fly to Pakistan for a wedding. But why, I wondered. Why spend that money on what is essentially a party? Marriage under Islamic law, as well as most civil laws, required only two things: a contract between the bride and groom, and a public announcement to let the wider community know that two families had joined. It was traditional for the bride and groom to stand together before an imam, in front of their family and friends, but it was not necessary. It was entirely proper, if uncommon, for a groom to be married through a proxy — that is, to have someone stand in for him and sign the papers on his behalf. It was not at all romantic, but it was practical. Anyway, I reasoned, wouldn't it be more romantic to start our lives with a few extra dirhams?

On January 3, 1975, my family and a dozen or so of Ghazala's relatives gathered at her house in Faisalabad. She wore a green three-piece *shalwar kameez* elaborately embroidered in gold, an homage to her mother who had worn gold stitched with green on her own wedding day. A traditional luncheon feast was served, goat meat and roast chicken and meatballs and rice and three varieties of vegetables. The local imam brought a brief two-page contract that listed our names and birthdays, our witnesses and parents, and the amount of the dower I paid, which was a little more than thirty-two rupees, or about $14 in today's American money. (The dower is often a token, a small sum paid to make the contract legal and binding, though it has also been perverted at times into an outright brokerage fee, rich men buying young brides for outrageous sums in transactions sanctioned by mullahs with a curious interpretation of Islam.) There was a notation, too, that "in case of disagreement" I would provide Ghazala a house and five hundred rupees a month, though we were confident that no such severe discord would arise. Every bride and groom would be on their wedding day.

The ceremony itself was straightforward. The imam asked Ghazala, after she'd read the contract, "Do you consent to this?"

She said yes, and then the imam asked her twice more, as required, so that there would be no doubt.

I was at work that afternoon. I got a phone call at the office, and the imam asked if I accepted Ghazala as my wife. "Yes," I told him. "With all my heart." It was what I wanted more than anything else.

Ghazala signed the papers, and then my proxies — my father and one of my uncles — signed on my behalf. That was it. We were husband and wife, bound forever and yet a thousand miles apart, married over the phone. It was, truth be told, mildly disorienting, at once joyous and anticlimactic. I went to bed that night euphoric and lonely, a peculiar combination.

The next morning, Allen teased me. "Hey, everyone," he announced to the office. "Notice anything different about Khizr?" A pause for effect. "No?" Another pause. "He's a married man! Yesterday he was single, today he is married."

It was gentle teasing. Allen and Lisa were thrilled for us. My one-bedroom apartment, paradise to me, wouldn't do for a married couple, they said. So the day Ghazala was

151

scheduled to arrive — I'd arranged her visa immediately, but it still took a few days to get her on a flight — Lisa packed up everything that wasn't company property and moved it to one of Robray's two-bedroom units. Allen and Lisa also decided we should have a proper wedding night, that I shouldn't see my bride for the first time when she was tired and rumpled after a long flight. Traditionally, the bride's parents would escort her to the groom's home, but since that wasn't possible, they stepped into that role, not usurping familial authority but almost like proxies, the way my father and uncle had done for me. They would greet her at the airport, bring her into the city, give her time to rest and dress before sending me home to my bride.

I worked late that night, as usual, except I couldn't concentrate. I sorted papers and rearranged files, fidgeting, really, to keep myself busy. But how could I focus on anything but Ghazala? Allen and Lisa had taken flowers to the airport, and, because they knew all the officials there, were able to meet her as soon as she walked into the terminal. They got her through immigration and drove her to our new apartment, which I hadn't even seen yet. They got her settled, then left her alone to get ready.

A couple of hours passed, slowly. "It's time," Allen finally said. "Time to go home and see your bride."

I fumbled with the key to the Toyota, jittery with anticipation. I hadn't seen Ghazala in more than nine months. This was decades before the Internet, or even affordable international calling. We'd had no video chats because there was no such thing, and we had spoken by telephone only a handful of times. Mostly we wrote letters. I realize that seems hopelessly primitive now. But Ghazala has saved all of them, secreted away those yellowing cards and sheets of paper in a box, each still neatly folded into its envelope. Our grandchildren can read them someday, relive part of our story, which is their story, too. It's hard to put FaceTime or Skype in a box.

The new apartment was in a different building from the one-bedroom. It wasn't far from the office, and I knew the way, but it seemed to take a very long time. I parked, jogged up the stairs, stopped in front of the door.

I had no key. I had to knock to meet my bride.

Ghazala opened the door.

Her eyes were still as green.

We stood in the doorway for a moment,

the two of us looking at each other with a kind of wonder. She wore a traditional bridal gown, a long skirt with a loose, long-sleeved blouse, embroidered with almost magical detail, red and green and purple and orange, elaborate and delicate swirls and ribbons of color, all of it glowing against the softness of her skin.

She was there, finally. Real. In the flesh. In an instant, years cascaded through my memory: watching her on a bus, not even knowing her name; bumping into her on a sidewalk; twenty-one birds bought cheap at a market; the arguments she'd had with her mother. All of it had led to this moment in a company apartment in Dubai. My wishes and prayers tangled together, all of them racing back through the months, twining around each other, then collapsing into a singular instance of enormous, gratifying relief. My Ghazala was with me tonight, and she would be with me tomorrow and every day after.

I stepped inside and embraced her. "I am so sorry about your father," I said.

I realize, so many years later, in a different time and place, that those might seem odd first words for a young groom to say to his bride. But expressing condolences was the most important thing I could do at that moment. It was my way of honoring her father and showing my respect for how much she loved him. He had entrusted his daughter, the one who brought comfort to his eyes, to my care. Without him, we could not have been together.

"Your father asked me to promise that I would always take care of you, Ghazala," I said. "And I will. I promise you, I will."

She hugged me tighter. As I had done nine months before, Ghazala had left everything she'd ever known, had landed in a foreign country where nothing was certain and she knew no one except her new husband. If she was afraid, she did not let on. "Everything will be okay," she whispered. "Everything."

Our first child, a son, was born nine months later, in October 1975. We named him Shaharyar, which, depending on the emphasis in the pronunciation, means either a friend of the people in the city or a friend from the city. We stressed the syllables into the first meaning. He was welcomed into the family as a golden child, as the firstborn often is. He was a quiet, contented baby, doted on, adored. Our family was just beginning, yet already our lives felt whole.

Eleven months later, in September 1976,

Ghazala gave birth to our second child, also a son. We named him Humayun Saqib Muazzam Khan.

In classical Persian literature, there is a bird called a huma, which is said to live its entire life in flight, never alighting, endlessly soaring through the skies. To even glimpse one is the rarest of occurrences and considered a sign of good fortune. In one version of the story, to have a huma fly over you — to be a *humayun* — foretells ascension to the throne. Humayun's second name, Saqib, was suggested by Ghazala's mother. It means star. Taken together, his name proclaimed him a most fortunate child, destined for greatness, a king who would shine among the heavens.

The years that followed were peaceful, full of gratitude for what we had. Our young family was together, neither of our sons sent to live with his grandparents. Ghazala took to motherhood easily, with a calm patience that many young women with two babies in a foreign country might find difficult to maintain. I was making a decent living, enough to support us and still set some aside. My anxiety about the future, which had worn at me for so many years, gave way to a comfortable ease with the present.

Allen and Lisa left Robray to be the

general managers of an oilfield supply center, a compound that handled the equipment and personnel needs for a number of drilling companies. I eventually followed and took the title of personnel coordinator, which was basically the same job I'd been doing except now I had five people working under me: a Brit who did the hiring and firing, a couple of local Arabs we used as runners, and an Indian and an Egyptian who did most of the filing and organizing. The money was better, enough that we could afford to move into a three-bedroom apartment.

The one lingering frustration was my education. When Humayun was born, I could feel the hands of the clock begin to turn faster. In a blink, both boys were walking and talking, and in a few years they would be starting school; their needs would be the ones that mattered most, not mine. If I was going to get a degree, I would have to do it soon.

"I think I should apply to American universities," I told Ghazala one night after the boys had been put to bed. Shaharyar was always quick to fall asleep, but Humayun fussed a bit. If his diaper was wet or his clothes not wrapped just right, he would let us know, promptly and loudly.

"America?" she said. "I thought we would go to England."

"I thought so, too," I said. "But look at the people we've met, the difference between the Americans and the English."

She looked at me quizzically, but only for a moment. She had understood. Our American friends had shown exceptional warmth and openness, a generosity of spirit that was infectious. There was a fundamental appeal to Americans that is difficult sometimes for them to understand themselves. I used to tell a joke to the expats in my office to explain the difference. Two men, one from Tennessee and one from London, are sitting across from each other on a train when a third man boards. "Hey, I'm Bob," he says. "Can I sit with y'all?"

"Sure," the Tennessean says. "Where you from?"

"I'm from Kentucky," he says, "little town down near the border."

"Yeah? I'm from Tennessee! How 'bout that?"

The two Americans get to talking and they go on and on, long into the night. The Englishman sits there quietly, reading a book, dozing off. In the morning, Bob looks at him and says, very friendly, "Hey, you ain't had much to say. I'm Bob."

The Englishman stares at him for a moment. "I didn't say anything," he tells Bob, "because no one introduced me."

The joke may not be laugh-out-loud funny. But it always got a knowing nod in Dubai because that was the difference between Americans and pretty much everyone else. There was no pretense, no stilted propriety. Americans were genuine, unselfconscious. They'd speak the same way, I'd noticed, at a sports bar as they would at a family picnic or in a high-class restaurant. They were *real*. And to me and Ghazala and our boys, they had been universally kind.

"If they're like that here," I said, "if all those cowboys in a Muslim country can be so kind to us, imagine what they would be like at home. Allen could connect us with some people. And the schools are the best, right? The University of Missouri has a very good program in international law. And I thought I would apply to Harvard, too."

Ghazala brightened. "Really?" she said. "Harvard?" she said. We might not have known a lot about the United States growing up in Pakistan, but Harvard is a recognizable brand all over the world, the veritable Holy Grail of higher education. "Very good," she said. "Very ambitious."

I wasn't suggesting that we emigrate to

the United States. I was not on a quest to live in America, just determined to get the best education I could. Frankly, Ghazala and I had no idea where we would live after I'd gotten a degree, though we had concluded that neither of us wanted to return to Pakistan, at least not then. Ghazala already believed Bhutto's populism had run the country into the ground. But then, in 1977, Pakistan descended into utter chaos. Bhutto was deposed in a bloodless coup by General Muhammad Zia-ul-Haq (he would also arrange for Bhutto to be tried and executed two years later for purportedly arranging the murder of a political opponent), who declared another period of martial law and converted Pakistan into his version of an Islamic nation. A person's religion was noted on his passport, schoolbooks were purged of "un-Islamic" material, and workplaces were forced to offer places to pray and workers to obey the muezzin's call. The legal code was rewritten into medieval savagery: Whipping was a legitimate punishment, blasphemy a criminal offense. The mujahideen — the Islamic holy warriors — were given free rein to beat men in the streets for having insufficiently long beards.

This was not an Islam that I recognized, that most Muslims who studied the teachings of the Prophet, peace be upon him, would recognize. This was the politicized thuggery of frightened, desperate men, a deliberate perversion of religion in order to maintain control over an illiterate and oppressed population. The Islam I'd been taught could be distilled to that story of the last hajj, when the pious man gave up his food and water to the hungry widow and her children. I had come to believe that, at their root, most religions could be similarly condensed: Be kind and merciful to all, live as if the Creator is alive in each person. The rituals and dogma are merely guideposts, culturally specific markers to help the faithful maintain a righteous path. Properly applied, religious conviction can be a force for good, encouraging charity and compassion and reflection; or it can be used to dominate and terrorize, to force compliance with antiquated and barbaric rules.

Reading and hearing about what was happening to Pakistan, who would want to live in such a place? Who would willingly subject his children to growing up there? Certainly not anyone with a choice in the matter, which Ghazala and I had.

I thought of Allen's warm smile, his generosity. Yes, we would go to America, at least for a while.

■ ■ ■ ■

I applied to perhaps half a dozen schools in the United States. New York University, Columbia, UC Berkeley, Missouri. Harvard, of course, which offered a one-year LL.M. — it stands for the Latin for Master of Laws — program. I was not optimistic, but I would have been remiss if I hadn't at least tried to get in.

I requested an application, carefully filled it out, and then wrote the required essay. I'd developed good material during my years in Dubai, which was basically a fifteenth-century fiefdom sloshing into the modern age on a tide of oil money. That's what I wrote about: how to create a modern legal system in a rapidly developing nation, melding what I'd learned in the university in Lahore and in the bureaucracy in Dubai into a coherent and practical theory.

Weeks passed, maybe months. One day in the early winter of 1978, Jenny, the British woman who handled the mail at the oil supply center, brought my usual stack. In it was a plain envelope, postmarked Cambridge, Massachusetts. I closed the door to my office and opened the letter.

I read it once, then again to make sure I

understood.

Harvard had accepted me.

I folded the letter and put it back in the envelope. I didn't say anything to anyone that afternoon. When I got home, I showed Ghazala the letter. I've never been prone to euphoria, as perhaps I should have been at moments such as that. But my mind reflexively jumped from the immediate present to the tasks ahead, the money that would have to be saved, the logistics of moving a family — I couldn't leave my family — to another country, even temporarily.

"I think we can do this," I told Ghazala. "I think we can make this work."

In my memory, Ghazala reacted in a tone of equal practicality. "Yes," she said. "We should do this." In fairness, though, time might have flattened out the emotion: Ghazala remembers me coming home elated, almost giddy. "That was a very happy moment," she says now. "Very happy. That was everything Muazzam had worked for."

The next day, I found Allen in his office.

"I got into Harvard," I told him.

He looked up, beaming. "That's excellent," he said. "Congratulations." Then his face shifted, subtly rearranging into a look of concerned curiosity. "Are you going to

163

accept it?"

I shifted my weight. "I guess so," I said.

I was smiling, but Allen could tell from my voice that something was slightly off. The problem was, tuition was $10,000 a semester, the equivalent of almost $40,000 in today's money. I'd saved some, but not that much, and Allen knew it.

"Can you defer it?" Allen asked.

"Yes, I can. Until I have the money."

"That's okay, then," he said. "You'll get the money. Go to Houston. You've got connections with Robray there. You can get a job there, earn more money, save enough to pay for it." A pause. "You can't turn down Harvard."

No, I couldn't turn down Harvard. I knew he was right. Not being able to afford something — my law school exams, white doves at Tollinton Market, a hotel room in Dubai — had never stopped me before. I'd just have to work harder and hope everything fell into place. As my father always said, it would all balance out in the end.

CHAPTER 5
THE WONDERS OF THE DMV

I landed in Houston in late 1979 carrying a single silver Samsonite suitcase and $200 in my pocket, which is the kind of detail every immigrant remembers to include, decades after the fact, when he's telling the story of how he came to make a success of himself in America. But I didn't consider myself an immigrant. I was a student, or would be, and I believed that I would be staying only long enough to get my Harvard degree. I would have to work for a while, maybe a couple of years, to be able to afford the tuition, which would make me a resident. But I was then, and assumed I would continue to be, a citizen of Pakistan. We might not live there until the theocratic tide had receded, but it was still my country.

Also, in fairness, I had more money in the bank.

Houston, for me, was the capital of Texas, which might as well have made it the unofficial capital of America. Most of what I knew about the United States had been filtered through oilmen in their blue jeans and cowboy hats, and most of what I'd seen had been in photographs on Texas-themed calendars and posters tacked to office walls. For some people, maybe most people, New York City or Washington might better represent the country, might be firmer ground on which to anchor themselves. But I'd gotten comfortable with the expats in Dubai, many of whom came from some little town in that great big state, so I felt comfortable with Texas.

I'd flown with Ghazala and the boys to Pakistan, where they moved in temporarily with my parents. Relocating to a new country for an extended stay involves some logistical challenges — finding an apartment and a job, to begin with — and we decided that it would be easier for me to deal with those alone, without two toddlers in tow. Once they were settled, I got on a Pan Am flight through Munich that landed on a Friday afternoon in Texas.

Houston Intercontinental Airport was a huge, sprawling complex, dwarfing the little outpost I'd gotten so familiar with in Dubai. I moved with a stream of passengers toward the immigration desk, presented my papers,

166

passed easily through customs (I had nothing to declare because I pretty much had nothing, period), and emerged into a crowded arrival hall that was both cavernous and gleaming with modernity. Unlike the expat oil workers, who were almost uniformly white, Houston was a cosmopolitan city; there were white people and Hispanic people and Chinese people and people who looked like me and more black people than I'd ever seen in one place before. The proverbial American melting pot was on full display from my very first steps into the country. A brown-skinned man from the other side of the planet had landed in the heart of Texas, and no one in the multitudes even noticed, let alone looked at me funny, as if I were obviously out of place.

I didn't feel any particular sense of triumph, of accomplishment, no joyous relief. I realize, putting memories to paper now, that I'm violating the narrative rule of the American immigrant memoir. But America was not then the Promised Land to me. I had other, more immediate concerns, those being my education and my family. America was where Harvard happened to be, and where I could work long enough and hard enough to afford it. I was as practical-minded landing in Houston as I had been filing papers in Dubai or studying for my exams in Lahore. In retrospect, that is one of the magnificent things about the United States, that it would allow a son of Pakistani farmers to come and work and get the best education in the world. There are very few countries so accommodating, so welcoming. But my thoughts then were only that a door had been opened, and I had to figure out how to move through it, methodically, ploddingly. I had to get myself established, earn enough to bring my family over, and then earn enough more to go to school.

The first thing I had to address, though, was hunger. It was a long flight from Munich, and I was famished. I found a food court in the terminal, a line of brightly lit counters and kiosks, chains and local one-offs I didn't recognize. To one side, however, was a little stand selling hot dogs. I knew hot dogs. Allen used to organize cookouts for all the Robray employees with hamburgers — which I'd been fascinated to learn were not, in fact, made of ham — and pizza and hot dogs, always beef in deference to the number of Muslims the company employed. Allen was good like that, always propping up morale. Some nights, he'd rent out a conference hall in one of the expensive hotels and screen American movies; Ghazala and I had been amused to notice that Anthony Quinn in *The Guns of Navarone* looked a lot like my father, especially in profile, and his voice had the same tenor and pitch.

The hot dogs were two for a dollar, which I could afford, and I remembered how good they tasted when you were hungry. I usually had mine with just ketchup and mustard, but there was a large array of condiments, all set on a counter to the side. One of those was chili. I'd never heard of chili, but thought I should try it. I put neat lines of ketchup and mustard on one dog, and ladled chili on the other. It was delicious. Thirty minutes in America, and already I'd made a wonderful discovery. I've preferred chili dogs ever since.

My belly full, I went out to the curb to find a bus. My plan was to go to the University of Houston, where there would be student housing and, since I was basically a student myself, I might be able to find an inexpensive place to stay. I assumed the university would be near the city center, and looked for a bus going there.

I saw one idling at the curb, doors open, driver in his seat.

"Excuse me," I said. "Does this go to the city center?"

"Look at the sign," he said, pointing up and toward the front.

I leaned around, looked above the windshield. The sign said DOWNTOWN.

I turned back to the driver. "Yes?" I said, more question than answer. Why would the city center be called "downtown"? Wouldn't that be the part of the city below the center?

"Yeah," he half sighed.

I hoisted my Samsonite up the steps and took a seat. I spoke English fluently, but I was going to have to learn some new terms.

The University of Houston was not downtown. I got off the bus, asked a few strangers for directions, found a different bus, and got on that one. It was a pleasant ride, but longer than I'd expected, the city more spread out than it had seemed in tight calendar shots of shining towers. Those towers, too, were bigger in person, the perspective looking up from the ground more impressive than staring at a medium-distance photograph.

The bus dropped me off in front of a wide brick gate with UNIVERSITY OF HOUSTON spelled out across it, the first word on the left side, the next two on the right. I carried my suitcase through it and saw, to my right, a sign for the Bates College of Law (which has since been renamed the University of Houston Law Center). That was a good omen, I thought, a law student like myself being delivered directly to a law school. It was past five o'clock and the sky was washed with evening light, but the lights were still on in the Bates building. I decided that that was my best option.

The door was unlocked, and I found myself in a small reception area at the foot of a long corridor lined with office doors. There was a young man there, maybe a student or maybe staff; I never knew which, but he was the only person for me to approach.

I told him I had traveled from Pakistan and that I was looking for a room, perhaps a dormitory where I could stay for a few days.

"No, sorry," the man said. "Housing is a different office, on the other side of campus." He looked at his watch. "It's after five. They're closed now. Everyone's going to be gone."

We stood there talking for a few minutes, trying to figure out what I was going to do with night falling and my funds not sufficient for an expensive hotel room. As we talked, a man in a turban emerged from one of the offices. I recognized him as a Sikh.

He looked too old to be a student, so I assumed he must be a parent taking care of some paperwork for his son or daughter. He was walking past me at the same time my conversation with the young man had petered out.

"I see your suitcase," he said, motioning toward my Samsonite. "You must have traveled a long way. Where are you from?"

"I came from Dubai," I said, "but I'm from Punjab."

"Welcome!" he said in Punjabi. It's a language with the same roots as Urdu, and I'd picked it up fairly well when I was younger.

"Thank you," I said, also in Punjabi. I explained to him what I'd just finished explaining to the other man, that I was looking for a place to stay and had hoped I might find university housing.

"You can stay with me," he said, without giving the matter any thought. "Yes, come home with me, you can stay for the weekend, and I will bring you back here on Monday morning."

"Really?" I said. This appeared to be another coincidental blessing, perhaps the divine intervention I was hoping for. Twice I'd landed in foreign countries with little money, no contacts, and nowhere to stay, and twice strangers had given me shelter. But I do not believe that was purely luck. Each person, my faith teaches me, is here for a reason, and each reason is just as holy as another. Perhaps one man is destined to design tall, splendid office towers reaching to the sky, and perhaps another is destined to file the paperwork for the building permits. Neither purpose is less than the other, because neither can be fulfilled without the other. All of us are connected, woven into an unfathomable tapestry, each thin strand a necessary part of the whole. I believe every person, no matter his or her station, should be afforded the dignity of kings. It is possible, then, that generous strangers appearing when I desperately needed their help was not coincidence but design.

My new sardar ji friend — "sardar ji" being a title of respect for a Sikh — lived in one of Houston's ubiquitous subdivisions. We drove there on wide boulevards that slimmed down to quieter residential avenues, and I noticed that the pavement was both smooth and painted with tidy lines, yellow down the middle, white marking the edges. Every street was like that, and the full length of each, too, rather than haphazard and splotchy markings splashed onto just a few dozen feet of the road, the rest pitted and blank, as in Pakistan or Dubai. In the sardar ji's neighborhood, the lawns were bright green and neatly clipped, and so many flowers bloomed — pinks and purples and reds and whites and yellows bursting from the ground — that it seemed as if the entire city was a garden, the buildings set around the flora instead of the other way around.

I felt a sense of satisfied relief. To the extent that I'd imagined America, it was this, leafy and blossoming and clean. The streets were not paved with gold, but at least they were covered with a proper layer of well-marked asphalt.

I stayed with the Sikh for two nights. Over dinner on Friday, a delicious Punjabi meal of rice and lentils with pickles and yogurt, he suggested that instead of waiting until Monday to return to the university, he would take me to the Islamic Center on Richmond Avenue on Sunday. "There will be many people there," he said, "and I'm sure you'll be able to find what you're looking for."

I was happy with that change of plans. By Saturday evening, I was beginning to fear that I was imposing on their hospitality, and told my host as much. "Oh, no," he said, "not at all. We're honored to have you. Guests bring blessings into our home."

I was humbled. He was a complete stranger — I never even found out why he'd been at the law school, as I thought it would be rude to pry. But when he'd taken me to his home, he'd told his wife that he'd brought a guest. He'd been speaking in Punjabi and he used a specific word, *parona*. Roughly translated, it means a sort of blessed traveler who will be a guest for a short while. There is no direct English translation, nor, I suppose, does there need to be.

On Sunday morning, my sardar ji friend dropped me at a small, weathered house on Richmond Avenue that had been converted into an Islamic center. The interior walls had been removed, opening the first floor into a prayer hall, and there were a couple of modest offices for the staff and for people like me who might need to borrow a telephone. Sunday is not the major day of worship in Islam — that's Friday — but there were a few people inside, visiting and available to assist people, again, like me.

I introduced myself, said I was from Pakistan via Dubai, I'd come to study, and that I needed an inexpensive apartment to rent. As luck would have it, there was a complex of two-story brick buildings directly across the street with a FOR RENT sign hanging in the window of what appeared to be the office.

The manager was a plain, middle-aged woman with short blond hair and glasses who seemed pleased to have a prospective tenant knock on her door. She walked me down the sidewalk a few doors and unlocked a one-bedroom unit on the ground floor. It was small but clean and partially furnished and only $200 a month. I told her I would take it.

"It's yours, then," she said. "Let's go do the paperwork, and I'll give you the keys."

We went back to her office. I filled out the lease, paid her $100 in cash for the security deposit and $200 for the first month's rent with a check drawn on my Dubai account. She asked me, as a matter of course, for a photo ID. I gave her my Pakistani passport.

She eyed it curiously. "Is this all you got?" she asked.

I nodded. "I've only just arrived Friday," I said. "From Dubai, but originally I'm from Pakistan."

"Well, it'll do," she said. "But you're gonna need something more if you're gonna get around here. What you need is to get

176

yourself a driver's license."

"Oh, I have one. From Dubai."

"No, a Texas one. So people know you live here. You need to go down to the DMV and get your picture taken and put on a license."

I nodded again. I assumed DMV stood for "Something Motor Vehicles," probably Department. I asked the manager how to get there, and she gave me the number of the bus that, conveniently, would roll right down Richmond Avenue. So a few days later, I stood on the curb, waiting for a bus that pulled up at the exact minute it was scheduled.

This was a marvel of efficiency, a bus arriving on time. In Pakistan, if schedules existed at all, they were little more than random times listed on a sheet, meaningless. A bus came whenever the driver felt like it. That could be in ten minutes, or an hour, or two if the driver was particularly peevish, lazy, or jammed in traffic. It was impossible to plan your day around the whims of a bus in Lahore or Gujranwala. But in Houston, I could time my travels to the minute. If it was raining, I could wait in my apartment, checking my watch until the minute hand was two ticks from the scheduled arrival time; if I started walking then, I'd meet the bus exactly when it pulled to the curb.

Reliable bus service is something Americans take for granted, but it's a minor miracle for a newcomer from a developing country. You know what else Americans assume almost as a birthright? An address. The high-end urban areas and more well-off neighborhoods in Pakistan might have properly numbered houses, but the great masses used complicated directions instead. *Take a right at the big tree, then look for the house with the balcony. That's not it. Mine is in the next row, three to the left.* In theory, each plot of land had a number assigned to it and each street had a name, but the bureaucrats in charge of disseminating the signs and numbers faced a constant choice: Put up the hardware, or use that money to send my kid to London for the weekend or buy new furniture for my house or just put it in my wallet. In Houston, though, I lived on a street marked with a sign in an apartment with a number to which Ghazala could send letters and I could expect them to arrive.

And telephones! A day or so after I moved in, I asked the manager how I could get one installed. She raised a quizzical eyebrow. "You call the phone company," she said.

"And how long will that take?"

178

"Oh, I don't know." She shrugged. "A couple of days, maybe."

Days? In Pakistan, getting a phone installed might take three or four *years*. Unless you knew the governor, and then it still might be a few months.

I went to a payphone on the street, dropped in a dime, called the phone company, gave them my address. Sure enough, two days later, a van pulled up outside my apartment. A technician fiddled with a few wires inside, and left me with a telephone and a brand-new number. I couldn't afford to call Ghazala in Pakistan — this was decades before cheap long distance, let alone inexpensive international calling — but I had a number for local calls and emergencies. A small thing, I realize, a convenience thoroughly embedded in the routine of American life then, much like the cellphone now. But when you've never had it, when you've never even had access to such simple things, they are astonishing luxuries.

I rode the bus west on Richmond Avenue for a couple of miles, and it dropped me not far from a DMV office on the same street. I only needed to pick up the thin booklet of rules and regulations to study for a written test, but I had to take a number anyway and sit on a hard plastic chair with everyone else on their hard plastic chairs.

I had mused a bit, in coming to America, about the amendments I'd read so long before. Would there be monuments to them? Would there be a statue to the First Amendment standing on a corner, or a park with a designated free speech spot, like the one I'd heard about in London? I had not found one, but a testament to it played out in the newspapers every day. There was a presidential primary under way, and people said the most awful things about the candidates, even about the sitting president, and no one seized the presses. That seemed monument enough. I'd come from a place where I'd seen newspapers disappear for days after they'd printed something displeasing to the government, only to return with a massive picture of Ayub Khan, sparkling in his medals, on the front page.

Free speech, I thought while waiting in my plastic chair, had always seemed to me the most difficult of American rights, the one that required the most tolerance. If people could speak their mind, they were going to say things that were unkind and critical and downright offensive. Yet you — we, all of us — put up with all of the bad speech in order to maintain the right to counter it with good speech. (And, of course, good and bad are inevitably matters of opinion.) It was a mark of heroic bravery, and of confidence in their fellow citizens, that the Founders put free speech at the top of the Bill of Rights.

And what of the Fourteenth Amendment, my favorite since I'd first read it, the one that guaranteed equal protection under the law for everyone? I didn't know the history in detail then, but I was aware that it was ratified after the Civil War to grant citizenship to "all persons born or naturalized in the United States," an oblique reference to freed slaves. But the history wasn't necessary: I appreciated its plain-text meaning, that everyone, rich and poor, black and white, was to be treated the same as far as the law was concerned.

The DMV office was crowded, and the clerks were deliberate, methodical, slow. Eventually, I'd get the standard American joke about the slothful pace of the DMV. But then I paid more attention to the people around me, who were all shapes and sizes, all races and, I assumed, religions. And all of them waited patiently on their uncomfortable chairs. It occurred to me that this, in its dreary bureaucratic grind, was the

Fourteenth Amendment put into practice. In Pakistan, the people who wait are the ones who can't afford not to, which was most of us. If a man had, say, an electric bill for one hundred rupees and he could afford to pay one hundred and *twenty* rupees, he'd push his way to the head of the line, slip the clerk the extra twenty, and be done, ignoring the grumbling and dirty looks from the rest of us stuck waiting. In Houston, we all took a number. We all waited. Maybe most of the people found it unpleasant, sitting there with nothing to do. But to me, it was refreshing, almost exhilarating, being equal to everyone else.

My number was finally called. I collected my materials, took the bus home, studied, and returned a few days later. I passed the written and driving tests easily enough, a clerk took my picture, and I walked out with a Texas driver's license with my name, Khizr Muazzam Khan, printed on it.

I laughed to myself, remembering the same bureaucracy in Dubai. One of Robray's employees, an Indian man with an impossibly long name, had passed his driving test and given the examiner his name, spelling it slowly and carefully. "Too long," the examiner said curtly. "You're now Mohammed."

The Indian man came to see me right after, clearly distraught. "I can't be Mohammed," he said. "I'm Hindu!"

I took him back to the examiner's station and managed to get it straightened out, which required a fair amount of diplomacy so as not to suggest that one of the sheikh's functionaries had made a mistake. But the difference was striking. In America, I could be me, a Muslim man from the subcontinent, and still be treated exactly the same as everyone else.

Even before I got my telephone or my driver's license, I started looking for a job. I was a licensed Pakistani attorney with years of experience working for an international oil field services company, but I did not delude myself into holding out for employment that would match my résumé. My Pakistani license didn't allow me to practice law in the United States; I would need my Harvard LL.M. degree for that. More important, I didn't have time for a protracted job search. I needed money, and I needed it quickly. My first priority was to earn enough to bring Ghazala and the boys to Houston. Perhaps I wouldn't be making a salary commensurate with my self-anointed status, but so what? And who was

I to be anointing myself with a status anyway? The important thing was that we would be moving forward as a family, slowly, but together. And then I needed to earn enough to afford Harvard. I would take whatever job I could get, so long as it paid a fair wage.

My connection to Robray didn't work out. I found the office without much difficulty, but that's all it was, an office. The faraway place that sent me a thick coil of faxes every morning in Dubai was nothing more than a single room staffed by a middle-aged lady. She was very pleasant, but she had nothing to offer me. "We just process the paper-work," she told me. She didn't need another set of hands to put pages in the fax machine.

In a newsbox on the street, I found a little green magazine of classified advertisements — cars for sale, apartments for rent, and the like — appropriately called *The Green Sheet.* I flipped through it and, in the Help Wanted section, I found an ad for a small school about twenty minutes down Rich-mond Avenue that was looking for someone to manage the office and teach English to non-native speakers. I called the number from a phone in the Islamic center and scheduled an interview. I was hired on the spot, $3.50 an hour for forty hours a week.

It was a cramped space, just a classroom and a couple of offices surrounding a reception area, but it had a steady stream of immigrants wanting to learn. Mostly, I taught English, but I also answered the phones and organized the files. I was the hungriest employee, the one who came in early and stayed late and worked overtime if I could get it. Within two months I was promoted to manager, which was important not for the title but for the raise and the biweekly salary.

But I knew I could do more. The teaching job was from nine to five, which meant I was free from five to nine, sixteen hours. I needed only a few of those hours to sleep and eat. The rest, I could work. I found a second job downtown, in an office building next to One Shell Plaza, the tallest skyscraper in the city. I sat in the lobby from eleven o'clock at night until seven in the morning, keeping watch, stretching my legs outside in the glow of the Shell tower whenever I got drowsy. In the morning, I took a bus back to my apartment, showered, and took another bus to my teaching job. If the bus ran on time — and it always did — I could be home by six to sleep for a few hours before I took the bus downtown again.

Working those hours in those sorts of jobs is not uncommon among educated immigrants. The best estimates suggest that one out of every five college-educated immigrants is either unemployed or, more commonly, underemployed, Iraqi doctors selling shoes, Mexican chefs washing dishes, and the like. There are a number of reasons for that. Professional licenses don't always transfer, or visas might not be in order. But as a class, immigrants work, and they work hard. *Really* hard. Everyone who comes to America is seeking a better life. Maybe that means, depending on the person and the circumstances, to gain more political or religious freedom, or to escape poverty or war. But underlying that, in almost every case, is a desire for more economic freedom, a chance to earn more money and build a better life. It may not be the primary reason a person crosses the border, but it is the foundational one. I knew, like every immigrant, that America wasn't going to give me anything except opportunity. And opportunity is everything. But I was under no illusion that I wasn't going to have to earn it the hard way.

For months, my life was limited to working, sleeping, and living as frugally as possible.

My only indulgences were a cowboy hat, which seemed more of a requirement than a frivolity in Texas, and a car, an aging blue 1971 Chevy Impala, the same big American beast Will Wilkerson drove, that I saw parked on Richmond Avenue with a FOR SALE sign propped on the windshield. The old man selling it wanted two hundred bucks. Not dollars. *Bucks.* The oilmen in Dubai called dollars "bucks," too, and it always struck me as mildly amusing in its randomness. Why that word? How did anyone go from "dollar" to "buck," two words that have absolutely nothing in common? Very odd. Very charmingly American.

I later found out, for what it's worth, that the term dates back to the mid-1800s, when deerskins — buckskins, "bucks" for short — were used in trade on the American frontier.

I bought the least expensive insurance policy the Indian agent a couple of blocks down would sell me, and promised myself I would drive very cautiously. That had never been a problem for me. Allen used to tease me when I drove to his house for dinner. "Have you seen Khizr drive?" he'd say to the other guests. "You can't keep up with him! He's the fastest man on the road!" He'd say it with such exaggerated glee that everyone knew he meant just the opposite: I was a poky and exceptionally careful driver.

Ghazala and the boys flew in to Houston near the end of the summer of 1980. It was as joyous a reunion as one would expect, my beautiful wife and gorgeous boys by my side again. Time had dragged without them. They had come to visit for a few months earlier in the year, but now they were staying for good, the four of us together. Our apartment had rodents, and my work hours hadn't lessened, but all of my concerns — about the present and the future — were soothed just by having them with me.

I picked them up in my Impala and drove us all home to our small apartment. It was late afternoon, and we had just gotten all the bags inside when there was a knock on the door. I opened it and found an older white woman standing there. The smell of cigarette smoke hit me. She was holding two brown paper bags.

"Hello," I said, as much a question as a greeting. I recognized her as the woman who lived a few doors down with her husband. We'd never spoken, but I'd seen her outside smoking.

"Hi, I'm Paulette," she said. "I hope I'm not disturbing you, but I saw you with those two little boys and thought you might need some things. So I brought them."

She offered me the bags.

I was briefly speechless. Everyone I'd met in Houston had been friendly enough, but this was a deeply touching act of generosity and concern.

I took the bags from her. "Thank you," I said. "This is so very kind of you."

"Well, I thought they might be hungry," she said. "Let me know if I can do anything else."

"Yes, yes, I will. And thank you."

I closed the door and set the bags on the kitchen table. Paulette had brought milk and bread, butter and jam, a package of cookies, nothing extravagant, merely staples and simple treats. I looked at Ghazala, standing there in her traditional clothing, a scarf covering her head. She had a mildly stunned smile, her eyes wide with surprise.

In the grand scheme of things, Paulette's was a small gesture. Perhaps other Americans would have found it to be completely normal, a neighbor greeting new arrivals. But it had an enormous impact on both Ghazala and me. We came from a conservative, reserved culture where such spontaneous consideration would have been out of place. In Pakistan, a person moving in down the block would have been eyed with curios-

189

ity from a distance. Yet in my family's first moments in America — literally, *their first moments* — a virtual stranger had been concerned enough about their well-being to bring sustenance. Paulette didn't see a foreign woman in funny clothes, or a cocoa-skinned man infiltrating her neighborhood with his immigrant family. She saw two little boys and their mother, exhausted from a long flight and perhaps in need of some basic comforts she could provide. The groceries were not offered as a pretext, an excuse for Paulette to snoop or ask nosy questions, but rather as a sincere gift to weary travelers. I was not unaccustomed to the kindness of strangers, of course. The cabdriver in Dubai, Allen and Lisa, my sardar ji friend in Houston, had all been exceedingly generous. But their generosity was preceded by a personal connection, by directly interacting with me and recognizing both a common humanity and my immediate needs. Paulette, by contrast, had come unprompted. She could easily have stayed in her apartment, and I would have thought no less of her when I next saw her smoking outside.

There are many such minor customs and courtesies ingrained so deeply in American culture that most people don't even notice them. One day, for instance, Ghazala returned from the small grocery store up the street with a package of meat that she hadn't realized, when she paid for it, was pork. We don't eat pork, but couldn't afford to throw it away; we were living on a very tight budget, buying our bread from an outlet called Mrs. Baird's Bread Factory where a loaf that might cost a dollar in the grocery was only 25 cents.

"You can return it," I said.

"What?"

"Return it," I repeated. "You can do that here. Take it back and tell them you made a mistake and they'll let you exchange it."

"Really?"

"Yes, really." I understood her confusion. In Pakistan, returning a mistaken purchase was unheard-of. Not only was the customer not always right, as the saying goes, but he often was a nuisance; the average shopkeeper behaved as if he was doing you a favor by allowing you to buy his wares (which were extremely limited by American standards, too).

We also discovered preschool, which would not have been an option in Pakistan. We enrolled the boys that fall. They delighted in it, but Ghazala's mother, who was visiting us at the time, was perplexed and mildly annoyed by the projects they brought home, usually involving Popsicle sticks and finger paints. "What are they teaching my grandsons?" she wanted to know. "Why aren't they learning real things?"

Ghazala and I had no ready answer. So Ghazala went to the preschool and asked, not because she was concerned but because she wanted to know what to tell her mother. Miss Lovett, a young and pleasant lady who taught at the school, laughed, but in a gentle way that suggested she'd heard the question before. "We are preparing the ground," she told Ghazala. "Whatever seeds we plant now will grow later."

We relished her poetic answer, a premise in which I heard an echo of my own grand-mother's wisdom. Just as she believed that raising a child was contributing to the eternal community, the preschool, with its seemingly arbitrary crafts, was preparing our children, everyone's children, to become proper students. They were both invest-ments in children and, thus, investments in the future. Ghazala's mother was satisfied, and perhaps even charmed, by that explanation.

We continued our thrifty lives, slowly inte-grating into the ebb and flow of America.

The school where I taught English had sponsored me for a residency permit so that my family and I could legally remain. I used to look at my paycheck with curiosity, study all the deductions, the withholding for income tax and Social Security. I didn't see those as money being taken from me, but rather as a dutiful contribution to services provided to all residents. We paid; therefore, we belonged. We still didn't feel like immigrants, people who would settle here permanently, but we didn't feel like outsiders, either. We were content, which is a very good thing to be.

The boys started kindergarten at Frazier Elementary School, Shaharyar in 1981, Humayun the following year, Ghazala standing on the curb with a camera to memorialize the yellow bus that took them off for their first days. I worked my two jobs and earned enough that we could afford to take over the $450-a-month mortgage payment on a three-bedroom brick house the owner was giving up so he could move to Dallas. Just as Paulette had come with groceries, our new neighbors — who knew the previous owner — brought coolers stocked with milk and eggs and other such things to tide us over until our new refrigerator arrived. We were getting used to American generosity, but not to the point that we weren't touched and deeply thankful.

Assimilating was not difficult for us. It helped, of course, that we both spoke English. More important, though, I never felt that we were giving anything up, that we were being forced to subsume our culture, our identities, into something new and foreign. Instead, I focused on what we were gaining. Opportunity, for one thing, the chance to work hard and further my education, which was the reason we were in Houston to begin with. I'd been accepted earlier into a semester-long program in international law at the University of Missouri, and by the fall of 1982 I had saved enough to take a break from my jobs and enroll. While I was there, that program evolved into a two-semester LL.M. course, and, to my immense satisfaction, Ghazala and I were able to juggle the budget to allow me to finish most of the course work; I earned my degree after completing one final course in Houston the following summer.

More important, there was freedom.

I realize that sounds both simplistic and amorphous — *freedom* — like a lyric cribbed from one of those country songs I'd borrowed from Will Wilkerson. But I had twice lived under martial law. Freedom of speech and freedom of assembly are real and tangible things. There had been times in my life when getting arrested for saying the wrong thing or associating with the wrong people — or even just with too many people — had been a very real possibility. I'd seen police crack open the skulls of students who'd dared to simply march in the streets, listened as friends and scholars compared their bruises and welts and fractures like so many campaign ribbons. Their battle scars were not metaphorical.

And what was my future in Pakistan? To become a lawyer who *got things done*? Who knew which professional witness to call for an alibi? Or to be an honest attorney making modest wages, my integrity a professional millstone? Material success in my homeland, it often seemed, was commensurate with moral compromise.

But in Houston, in Texas, in America, I could sense endless possibilities. It's difficult to explain that feeling, that heady sense of a boundless future, but it's real. I'd left a place where my life was limited in unsettling and unsatisfactory ways for one where I was constrained only by my effort and desire and my ability to stay in the country. To ensure my good standing, I'd given myself two inviolable rules: always to pay my taxes and never to break the law — laws, I was quick to remind myself, written by legislators freely elected by the people and interpreted by impartial judges, rather than decreed by an autocrat and reinforced by corrupt functionaries who might just as easily be bribed into ignoring them. Generally speaking, there wasn't a cop in Pakistan who wouldn't take cash, who wouldn't let you get away with murder for a thick enough stack of rupees.

In America, however, there was a functioning civil order. I could see it in the mundane details, in the buses that ran on schedule down streets marked with clear, consistent signs, on the houses with proper numbers affixed beside the front doors, among the people who waited patiently, if grudgingly, at the DMV. It all operated under the umbrella of the grand American experiment, of the forefathers' insistence, and the Constitution's guarantee, that all men are created equal. I knew that as long as I didn't break either of my two rules, I would be left alone to pursue my own happiness. We were embracing, and embraced by, a universal aspiration.

But it wasn't all social studies and legal theory that made fitting in relatively easy for us. We were blessed with fine neighbors who warmly accepted us. There was, I'd realized years earlier in Dubai, a distinctly American personality, fine-tuned along the edges of each individual but at its core open and welcoming and gregarious. No one, so far as I was aware, looked at us with any hostility, as if we were interlopers, as if we didn't belong. There was only one time that I remember any obvious difference was even remarked upon.

Ghazala was pushing a mower across the lawn in front of the house, dressed, as she almost always is, in traditional clothing. She wore loose trousers and a long, billowy top. One of the neighbors watched her for a few moments, then waved to get Ghazala's attention.

"Can I ask you something?" she said. "Why do you wear those clothes?"

Ghazala recognized it as an honest question, not a thinly disguised jab. "Well," she said, "why do you wear *those* clothes?" She swept her hand, gently and gracefully, toward our neighbor's shorts and T-shirt.

"Um, because they're comfortable, I guess."

"Yes, of course," Ghazala said. "And that is why I wear these clothes."

The neighbor cocked her head, her mouth curled into a little half smile of understanding. "Huh," she said. "Yeah, that makes sense."

Ghazala smiled back and started pushing the mower again, just another Texan cutting the grass and tidying the yard, taking pride in her American home. And that's how we felt in those years. We were neither Texans nor Americans, yet we'd never felt so at home belonging to no place at all.

Outside Punjab University Law College, Lahore, Pakistan (circa 1972). I was twenty-two.

Ghazala when I first met her (1972). She was twenty-one.

Ghazala (front row, center) as captain of the all-girls netball team, after winning a championship trophy

Ghazala's
passport photo
(1970)

Ghazala outside her dorm (1972)

At the Ravi River in Lahore (1970)

Our first photo after she joined me in Dubai (1975)

Our first outing at Dubai Beach (1975). Dubai was
not so crowded then.

Dubai Beach (1975)

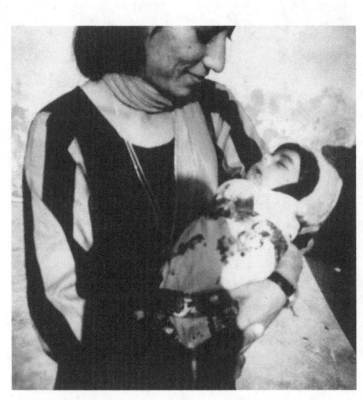

Ghazala holding her nephew, then recently born (1972).

Outside the entrance to Harvard Law School,
Cambridge, Massachusetts.

White Mountains, New Hampshire (1986)

At the Charles River, with Boston in the background (1985). I am holding Omer, age one.

Ghazala and Omer at the Charles River (1985)

A family picnic at Lake Houston, with Ghazala in a cowboy hat, Humayan (at left), and Shaharyar (1980)

We took turns wearing the cowboy hat.

Showing off our first baseball caps and Texas cowboy hat

Shaharyar (left) and Humayun (right) with
a neighbor friend (1980)

Humayun and
Shaharyar
outside the
Houston
apartment
(1980)

At the wedding of Ghazala's younger brother,
Abid, in Houston, Texas (1984)

The family in South Boston (June 1986). I am holding Omer, with Humayan next to me and Shaharyar at right.

At the Washington Monument in Washington, D.C.,
in July 1986—our first visit—with Omer, Shararyar,
and Humayun.

CHAPTER 6
ALREADY AMERICAN

In the mosque one Friday afternoon, Ghazala finished her prayers by touching her hands and head to the floor a final time, then straightening but remaining on her knees. She turned her head toward her right shoulder, where the angel who records one's good deeds is believed to perch, and whispered, *"As salam alaykum was rahmatullahi was baakatuhu"* — May the peace, mercy, and blessings of Allah be with you. She turned toward her left shoulder, where the angel who records one's misdeeds sits, and softly repeated the same phrase, ending her prayer ritual.

"Allah will not accept your prayers."

Ghazala looked to her right. A woman, older, Pakistani, was staring at her.

"Excuse me?"

"Allah," the woman repeated, "will not accept your prayers."

Ghazala gave her a confused look. "What

199

do you mean? Why do you say that?"

"I mean Allah will not accept your prayers."

Now Ghazala was somewhat offended, this stranger pontificating on Allah's intentions and her worthiness in His eyes. "Well," she countered, "how do you know He will accept *your* prayers?"

"I don't," the woman said. "But I know he will not accept yours."

As she spoke, she shifted her eyes to Ghazala's forehead and raised her own eyebrows in a self-satisfied way. Ghazala reached up, felt her scarf. It had slipped while she was praying, exposing a bit of her fine chestnut hair. Her head had not been properly covered as she finished *salaat.*

Ghazala was still bothered by that conversation when she recalled it for me later in the day. She wasn't concerned that her scarf had slipped. Her thoughts were on her prayers, not on a minor cosmetic malfunction, a consequence of the physics of bowing her head to the floor. She was upset, instead, that a person had taken it upon herself to interpret and declare the will of the Creator, that someone would be so arrogant as to presume Allah's will and condemn another human for a perceived failing.

It reminded us both of what we had left behind in Pakistan, or, rather, what Pakistan had become.

We already had been thinking of living permanently in America. We spoke openly of it in front of the boys, of the trade-offs and choices. We had friends and family in Pakistan. Generations of our ancestors were buried in its soil. There was a primal pull of home, as if our roots had stretched but not been completely severed from the other side of the earth. We could probably do fairly well for ourselves in Pakistan, too. If I bent myself to the system, or at least did not push too hard against it, I would in time be a successful attorney. Ghazala, whose Durrani lineage still carried some weight, would be an exceptional professor.

Without fail, however, those possibilities were dismissed. We agreed that we were in a better place in our brick house on Little River Road with the used Impala in the driveway. We just knew it. Sometimes, even if you can't say why, you know when you're home.

We kept up with the troubling news from Pakistan. General Zia-ul-Haq's Islamization of the country was complete, with tens of thousands of religious conservatives in-stalled in the bureaucracy, courts using deliberately deformed rules to adjudicate commingled matters of religion and jurisprudence, new rules and laws policed and enforced with the same arbitrary arrogance of that woman in the mosque deciding whose prayers Allah would accept. The Islam of tolerance and dignity, the Islam I had learned and embraced, that had been handed down to me by generations, had been replaced with a brutal theocracy. Yet for all the piety, corruption was still rampant. Even if Ghazala and I could tolerate such a morass, how could we subject our children to it? Humayun and Shaharyar had come to America when they were four and five years old. We'd been in Texas for four years already. They knew Dubai only in scattered, snapshot memories, and Pakistan only as the place where relatives lived.

Our boys were growing up as Americans. They were in a place, Ghazala and I always agreed, that was more compassionate, more welcoming, more tolerant, than the places we had left. Than anywhere else we'd ever been.

"We're going to become citizens," I told them one night in the mid-1980s, Ghazala beside me, the two of us confident in our decision. "We're going to stay in America."

They did not visibly react, probably because to them that announcement would have carried the same weight as *I'm going to work* or *We need to buy milk.* I don't think they ever expected we would leave the only place they really knew. For years, in casual conversations, whenever it was appropriate to bring it up, we'd talked to them about civil liberties, about the freedoms America guaranteed. Often, those were intertwined with discussions of faith. Islam emphasizes the equality of all humans — the Qur'an always speaks to "O Humankind" — and teaches adherents the imperative of treating each person with equal dignity. In America, those same basic teachings were established in the founding documents. "I know a scholar of Islam," I would tell them, "a very learned man, very devout. And he told me once that in Pakistan, I read about my religion but did not find it. Then I came to America, and I was able to find it here."

In theory, we could have applied to stay indefinitely as permanent legal residents. In practice, that status would have been revocable at some point in the future. And as resident aliens, we would always be just that — aliens, strangers in a strange land, even if that was not at all how we felt. As citizens, though, we would be fully invested in America, and America in us. We would have great privileges, *certain inalienable rights,* and the opportunity to exercise their commensurate responsibilities. Those laws I promised never to break? If there was one I believed was unjust or erroneous, I could vote for a representative who might help change it. I could have voted for Ronald Reagan, whose sunny view of America aligned with mine and, judging from his landslide victory in the 1984 election, that of most Americans; I'd been so taken by his speeches, his poetic embrace of the best of this land, that I carried in my wallet a Republican Party membership card with his signature on it. I would be able to petition my government for a redress of grievances, should I have any. We could speak freely and assemble with whomever we chose and be free from unreasonable searches and seizures and never be forced to give testimony against ourselves or have our property seized without just compensation. We would be equal under the law to everyone else. We would be guaranteed basic human dignities that millions upon millions of people all over the world would sacrifice dearly to have. Granted, noncitizens enjoy many of those same freedoms while they're on American soil, but as citizens we would own them, be part of the body politic responsible for protecting and defending them.

It was not a difficult decision. We wanted to be Americans.

And there was one more reason: Ghazala was pregnant. Our third child would be a citizen by birth. He would be wholly American. It seemed only proper that his parents earn that same privilege for themselves.

A security guard was posted outside the door to the immigration office. I showed him my letter from the government telling me to arrive at that place on that date to take my citizenship exam, and he waved me through the door.

I went inside to a reception area not unlike the one where I'd gotten my driver's license: hard plastic chairs, people of many colors and nationalities patiently waiting. I'd been in Houston for a little more than five years, the statutory minimum before I could apply for citizenship. A few months earlier, right at the demarcation point on the calendar, I'd filled out my application, mailed it in, and then gotten myself a booklet to study. Even though I was a lawyer, fluent in English, and knew basic American civics, the citizenship exam was sacred to me. Failing it was not an option I was prepared to consider. I felt as if I were crossing a bridge, desperately hoping it wouldn't collapse beneath me.

A middle-aged man in short sleeves came to the end of a corridor that emptied into the waiting room. "Khizr Khan?" he said. He came close to pronouncing my first name correctly — in English, it's *Key*-zer — but I heard "Khan" clearly. I stood up quickly, smoothed my tie, and buttoned my jacket. My exam was a serious occasion, and I'd dressed accordingly.

The examiner waved for me to follow him down the hallway to his office, a small, nondescript room with a desk and a pair of filing cabinets. "How are you, Mr. Khan?" he asked as he settled into his chair and motioned for me to take the one in front of his desk.

"I'm fine, and thank you for asking," I said. "How are you?"

That was more than me being polite. *I'm fine* would have sufficed, but I knew that he was gauging my ability to communicate in English, and extending a conventional courtesy was important. My study guide had suggested I speak like an acclimated American.

"Are you ready to take this test?"

"Yes, sir," I said. Respect for authority couldn't hurt, either.

"Okay, I need you to stand." He told me to raise my right hand, which I did. "Do you swear or affirm that the statements you will give today will be the truth, the whole truth, and nothing but the truth?"

"I do."

I sat back down when he did, and put my hands in my lap.

"All right, then, Mr. Khan, I just have a few questions for you," the examiner said. His tone was perfunctory, the voice of a man who went through this exercise dozens of times each week. How strange, it suddenly occurred to me, that the moment on which so many people's lives can pivot, the conversation that can deliver all the promises of the future, could become a matter of bureaucratic routine. "How many judges are on the Supreme Court?"

"Nine."

"Okay, very good. And who is the president of the Senate?"

A change-up, almost a trivia question. Most Americans have no idea the Senate even has a president. "The vice president," I said. "Mr. George Bush currently."

"Uh-huh. And how do you remove a judge from the Supreme Court."

"You cannot," I said. "They have lifetime tenure."

That was not technically correct. Supreme Court justices do have lifetime appointments, but they can be impeached. That has happened only once, however, to an associate justice named Samuel Chase in 1805, and he was acquitted in the Senate. As a practical matter, though, I wasn't really wrong. And, in any case, the examiners had fairly wide discretion back then (the civics exam was standardized in 1986 to ten questions, of which six are required to be answered correctly; I was asked only those three questions.) The point of the interview wasn't so much for me to pass an academic quiz as it was to see how well I grasped the basic ideals of America. Demonstrating a working knowledge of civics, and an ability to communicate clearly, was enough.

"All right, Mr. Khan," the examiner said, sliding a sheet of paper across the desk toward me. "I need you to read this out loud, so I can hear you."

There were three typed lines on the page, the same oath I'd sworn at the beginning of the exam. I read them aloud.

"Now I just need you to sign at the bottom."

I borrowed a pen and signed my name.

"Congratulations, Mr. Khan," he said, pushing his chair back and extending his hand for me to shake. His tone was still blandly official. "You'll get a letter telling you where to go for the citizenship ceremony."

I stood, shook his hand. Already he was gesturing toward the door, moving one soon-to-be citizen off the assembly line to make room for the next. I buttoned my coat, thanked him, and made my way down the corridor, through the waiting room, and out into the Houston heat. The security guard was still posted at the door.

I had to go back to work. The boys would be home from school soon. I was still scrambling to save money. The usual drone of the city, the traffic and pedestrians, all moving through their American lives, hummed around me.

Nothing had changed, and yet everything had changed. I thought of a word from my native language, *mahrum.* It means, in one context, a state of deprivation, not of food or material goods, but of the soul, of the heart. That moment, standing in a parking lot outside a drab government building in Texas, was the end of my being *mahrum.*

A rush of emotion came over me, almost as if, for years, I'd barricaded certain feelings behind a dam of doing, of working, of striving. Now I felt as if a dream had come true, which was almost overwhelming because I hadn't consciously realized I'd had this dream. A new and blessed country, one I could still remember reading about when it seemed a faraway fantasy land, had taken me in, had accepted me as one of its own. I'd found a home I didn't understand I was looking for.

I was going to be an American.

No, I realized, standing in a drab parking lot in the Texas heat, that wasn't it. As far as I was concerned, I already was an American. In my heart, I had been for years.

CHAPTER 7
NO MAN IS COMPLETE UNTIL HIS EDUCATION IS COMPLETE

The police came through the Public Garden on foot around midnight, their usual schedule, a pair of Boston officers patrolling together. I heard them coming, the two of them talking, their radios chirping, before they noticed me half-prone on the bench. I pivoted on my hip, swung my feet to the pavement, sat upright. The trick in those hours, late enough to fall asleep but too early for the cops to disappear, was to keep my shoes on. That saved a few seconds, enough to let me transform myself into an ordinary man enjoying the cool of the Boston night, instead of a shoeless hobo camping out on a bench.

The police walked past. I smiled and gave them a brief, greeting nod, but they didn't seem to notice me. I watched them walk away, slipping from one puddle of lamplight to the next, fading into faint silhouettes.

This was only my third night in the park,

but I'd learned the routine quickly enough. After the midnight pass, the police came through again a little after two o'clock in the morning, when the drunken tourists spilled out of the *Cheers* bar on Beacon Street, at the north end of the Public Garden. After that, I could take my shoes off and close both eyes, get a few hours' rest. The breaking dawn would wake me, and I'd slip my shoes back on before the morning patrol came through. If the police saw me then, they'd stop, ask me if everything was okay, which I suspected was more out of concern for the park and the public than for me.

"Oh, yes, fine, fine," I'd say, stretching but not moving with a guilty quickness, as if I'd been caught doing something wrong like, say, sleeping in the park. "I'm on my way to work and just stopped to stretch out my back a little." That was not wholly untrue; one's back did indeed get stiff catnapping on a bench.

The police would size me up, decide I was neither a vagrant nor a public menace. "All right, then," they'd say. "You have a good day."

Or maybe they wouldn't stop at all, a possibility I considered as I watched the midnight cops disappear into the darkness.

Maybe I'd get an extra hour of uninterrupted sleep.

I got up and walked south past the big bronze statue of George Washington astride a horse and standing like a sentry at the Commonwealth Avenue gate, to find a bench farther away from *Cheers.* Moving around was a practical precaution, making me look less like I was loitering, more like just another man sitting in the park. I swung my feet up, gently pushed off my shoes, left them at the end of the bench; even if I wasn't wearing them, it was still worth keeping them close. I lay back, rested my head on the hard arm of the bench.

I'd been in Boston for more than a year. I'd left Houston not long after my citizenship exam, when our youngest son, whom we named Omer, was two months old, to finally study at Harvard. I'd gotten my second LL.M. degree a month earlier, officially stamped with the Harvard Law School seal of approval, the most prestigious brand in the legal profession.

I squirmed, wriggled, rearranged myself to keep the slats from pinching my back.

I'd gotten a job the day after graduation, reviewing mortgage documents, tedious work, more suited for a file clerk than a lawyer. I imagine I could have found a position at a white-shoe law firm, sent my résumé around, gotten my suit cleaned and pressed for interviews. I had the pedigree, the experience. But searching for those jobs required time, a luxury I did not have. I needed a paycheck, immediately. We'd been living off our savings, and my year at Harvard had cleaned them out. Tuition, a cheap apartment in suburban Medford, books, bus fare, food. And that was just in Boston; in Houston, we had a mortgage payment and three boys to feed and clothe and entertain. Our only luxury had been when they drove the Chevy up from Houston for a visit during New England's short, wet spring.

The iron arm of the bench dug into my skull.

After I graduated, I'd rented a basement room for a few weeks in Allston, one of the grungier neighborhoods in Boston, crowded with college kids. It was damp, dark, and impossibly noisy. I had to move. I found a new room to let on a Friday, but the landlord needed a security deposit and a week's rent in advance. I didn't have it. I knew the family budget down to the penny, and there was nothing to spare; I sent Ghazala my entire paycheck, except for the $10 I always kept in the bank to avoid incurring service fees.

A breeze riffled the pond where the swan boats were huddled against the dock, a hulking flock of make-believe birds nesting in the shadows. Silver light caught the ripples, flashed, disappeared in the dark water.

Ghazala didn't know where I was sleeping. Why would I tell her? She would insist that I pay the deposit, I would refuse, and then she would worry. My burden would become her burden. Hadn't there been enough burdens? All the scrimping and saving and moving, from Pakistan to Dubai to Houston, away from everything and everyone we knew, had been for *my* education, for *my* benefit. My family could not possibly have done more to support me. How could I ask them to go without anything, even for a week or two? Ghazala and the boys would always come first, *must* come first. Their needs and their comfort were more important than my temporary inconvenience.

One more check, with overtime, and I'd have enough for the deposit. Six more days.

The boughs of the trees were black against the sky washed pale by the lights from Beacon Hill and Back Bay and, a little farther south, the Financial District. I hadn't slept outdoors since I'd left Pakistan, where I'd done so surrounded by the walls of my grandparents' courtyard. Back then, when I was a boy, I liked to stare up at the moon, watch it crawl across the sky. But if there was a moon rising over Boston that night, I couldn't yet see it, and I was too tired to wait.

Harvard is an almost mythical and allegorical place, like the Pentagon or Buckingham Palace. You know they all exist, that they are physical places, and maybe one day you will see them, walk in their hallways and on their greens. But until that moment, they are primarily concepts, their names shorthand for something larger, "Pentagon" a stand-in for American military might, "Buckingham Palace" for British royalty.

The name "Harvard" carries the same kind of weight, the idea of educational excellence distilled into seven letters; a graduate will inevitably have the phrase "Harvard-educated" in the first paragraph of his obituary. For me, it had been that even more than the place to which I'd aspired, that had been just out of my reach for years. Late at night, in the glow of the Shell tower, I would stretch my legs on a Houston sidewalk, blink the sleep out of my eyes, remind myself why I was working those two jobs. I was going to Harvard.

I flew to Boston in June 1985 and found a hotel room I could afford in Brighton, just across the Charles River from Cambridge. The next morning, I walked to Harvard Square, stepping through an unruly whir of traffic on an awkward weave of streets, and passed though one of the gates in the brick wall surrounding the old yard of the university. I stopped for a moment. The morning was cool, and dew was still on the grass. Scholars had walked these paths for centuries, and their presence infused the air. Giants of American history — John Adams, John Quincy Adams, Theodore and Franklin Delano Roosevelt, John F. Kennedy — had studied here, had opened the same doors I was about to open.

No man is complete until his education is complete.

Completing my education, however, was not inexpensive. I found my way to the registrar's office and paid my tuition for the semester, the first of two required for my Master of Laws degree. I wrote the largest check of my life, for $10,000, or about $23,000 in today's dollars, and there was still another semester to come. That check was, in the most literal sense, a massive investment in my future. I'd put all my money on the safest bet I could conceive of: myself.

I found an apartment I could afford that was a long bus ride away, bought the books I'd need for my first classes. A few days later, I was in one of the large lecture halls for orientation. I can't remember who spoke, someone from the faculty, and he said the usual thing, congratulating us on how much we'd accomplished just by being admitted, then reminding us, in a way that was both encouraging and ominous, that our fate from there on out was in our own hands, dependent solely on our own effort and discipline.

I looked around the room as he spoke. There were students from all over the world, black and brown and white and Asian. Eventually, I'd learn in whose company a farmer's son from Gujranwala had found himself. A few seats over sat an olive-skinned man whose brother was the president of Guatemala. Two rows up was Iqbal's daughter-in-law. The ambassador from Papua New Guinea was behind me, and to my left was a black man who, I would discover, was preparing to become the chief of the Masai tribe in Swaziland. It was just as well that I didn't know who any of them were then, though. At that moment, we were all equals, our status leveled by the egalitarianism of academia.

There was a lot of reading required: three hundred pages for this class, four hundred to prepare for that lecture, five hundred for the next seminar. But I was in my element. I was a student by nature, and the humbling I felt arriving at Harvard never morphed into intimidation. I was confident in my abilities, and, just as I'd been when I was a schoolboy in Pakistan, unafraid to stand up in class and speak my mind, which usually had a different tilt from those of my peers and professors. My classmates were an eclectic lot, but it is not unreasonable to say that I came from a different background than most. My perspective was not the same as that of the plutocrats or the management caste or, for all my studying, even the academic set who understood the world only in terms of competing theories. I was a child of the proletariat, of postcolonialism, of people who had to work in order to eat, who understood viscerally that the rich and powerful lived differently from the rest of us because I had suffered their edicts and whims.

Also, I liked a vigorous debate. I developed a reputation as the voice of the academic opposition.

Abram Chayes taught my favorite class, International Legal Transactions, a topic about which I'd developed strong opinions. I'd read a book early in the semester, probably for Chayes's class, about (as I interpreted it) the maltreatment of Third World countries by the extraction industries, the mining conglomerates and the oil-and-gas behemoths. It infuriated me. In country after country, a small cohort of elites, often members of a puppet government installed with the assistance of those same companies, enriched themselves at the expense of the masses. Why should a handful of people be allowed to sell off a nation's wealth for personal gain? I came to believe that almost all of those contracts were illegitimate as a matter of principle, if not of international law. On the other hand, I also believed in OPEC, the right of oil-producing countries to organize, to band together against the oil companies. (The complication that most OPEC nations were run by autocrats was not lost on me, but it didn't negate the basic argument.)

Chayes would lecture on a point of law or a particular case and then, with some regularity, would pause and gesture toward me. "And now," he would say, "let's hear from our socialist friend." I would oblige. It got to the point where classmates would ask me, "What do you have against everybody?"

Nothing, of course. I was *for* everybody, and against only those rapacious few who happened to control too much of the planet. I was not, however, a socialist. I believed as strongly as anyone in the value of hard work, in the necessity of individual effort. I'd been a night watchman, a teacher, and a personnel clerk to pay for Harvard.

Chayes wasn't baiting me out of belligerence. Instead, I was being coached to speak my thoughts aloud, hone them into proper arguments. An opinion isn't an argument until you practice it. I jousted, too, with Dean David Smith, another man I held in great esteem, in his class on Third World Mineral Rights. Harvard encouraged that kind of intellectual discourse. I also audited Lawrence Tribe's class on Constitutional Law — my required courses were drawn from a set list, but missing Tribe's seminar would have been like going to the Louvre and skipping the Mona Lisa — and watched as he pointed to unsuspecting students and posed wildly counterintuitive questions. "You," he'd say. "Tell me what was wrong with *Brown v. Board of Education.*" Explain why a landmark decision desegregating education, widely considered one of the

221

triumphs of twentieth-century jurisprudence and social progress, was flawed? Most people would reflexively answer that there was nothing wrong with it. But most people weren't being trained at Harvard, where those sorts of intellectual exercises were a routine part of the curriculum. (The most common critique of *Brown* was that the legal ruling had unintended, and significantly disruptive, social consequences, though I suppose that's more of a sociological than a legal point of view.)

For a year, I learned to think critically, logically, precisely, and how to express those thoughts properly. "Citations!" I can still hear the late Dean Frederick Snyder exhorting in his Legal Pedagogy class. "Without citing it, it's plagiarism. Do not ever commit plagiarism!"

It was an invaluable education, during which I often would find my mind wandering back to my childhood, to the stories my grandfather told. One night's recitation had been a particular line from Rumi. "Love stole my prayer beads," he said, "and gave me a song and a beating heart." It was cryptic, in the way that poetry often is to a young boy, and I lay awake under the moon, turning the words over in my head. I pondered it for days, then off and on for weeks, years. I'd decided Rumi meant he would think not only with his head, but also with his heart. And isn't that what Iqbal had explicitly written? "I have untangled the knots of the threads of wisdom — I want to think through my heart."

Those two impulses met at Harvard, converging into a single current. I could think with my brain. I could analyze and argue. I could be abstract and counterintuitive and, if required, contrary. But what good is a brain if it is not buttressed by a heart, by a conscience? I had come from a place so different from where I'd arrived. I knew what it was like not to have the blessings of America as a birthright, what it was like to live without rights, without dignity. All people want to live with dignity, and that so many do not is one of the things that makes dignity so precious. The American forefathers, the men who signed their own death warrants when they put their names to the Declaration of Independence, had codified those dignities in the Constitution and the Bill of Rights. The poets I'd read on the other side of the world had put them only into verse. So many of the poems I remembered could be distilled to a single true thought: *I, the Creator, have created all this, all of you, and all with dignity. Be kind to one another, and do not destroy what I have created.* But that didn't make them real the way law does.

My studies kept me occupied, but I missed my family terribly. If I dwelled on it, on how far away they were and how many months would still need to pass before we could be reunited, the longing became a physical pain. I remembered being separated from my parents, the evenings I'd weep on a hill on the side of the road, watching the bus lumbering off toward the horizon. I would never wish that on another child, let alone my own.

Houston was not always as hospitable to the boys as it had been to Ghazala and me. We had lovely neighbors, but the older boys were now in elementary school. Except for a pair of Vietnamese kids, they were the only ones who weren't white, and children can be terribly cruel. Our sons were different, and were often reminded of that fact. On the bus, older children picked on them so mercilessly that Ghazala began driving them to and from school each day. At Christmas, Shaharyar and Humayun would be called to the principal's office, the two Muslim students, to watch a video while all the other students exchanged small gifts at a party.

The adults meant well, trying to be sensitive to cultural differences, but all a child knows is that he's been singled out and sent to the principal's office.

They weren't completely isolated. Ghazala's sister and brother-in-law had immigrated to Houston with their five children, and then one of her brothers, his wife, and their three children. They came for the same reasons we did, for a life better than what Pakistan offered. And then her mother came, in 1982, because her children were here. Demographers call this pattern *chain migration,* one family member — me, in this case — blazing a trail for others to follow. But their cousins weren't in the same neighborhood, so mostly my boys had only each other.

Shaharyar and Humayun were as tight as twins. They were only a year apart in school, so they played together at recess and ate lunch together and shared the same small group of friends. "Alone, you are only one," Ghazala used to tell them. "But when you stand together, you're like the number 11." The boys would giggle because that didn't really make sense except in a Dr. Seuss kind of way, but they understood the point: Together, they had the strength of ten boys, plus one.

They both were good students. Just as my grandparents had instilled a respect for education in me, Ghazala and I tried to do the same with our children, methodically, repetitively. Once they were able to read, we required them to do so every day — and then to write a report on what they'd read, which we would discuss over dinner. This was not, to be honest, their favorite meal of the day. ("It's hard to be a kid," our oldest confessed years later, "and dread dinner.")

They had their different intellectual gifts. Shaharyar was logical, studious, the one who would grow into a true scholar, a scientist. Humayun was more empathetic, able to understand people, what made them tick. On Halloween night when he was in fourth grade, for instance, Humayun came home with an enormous sack of candy. But he didn't eat it. He just left it in his room. For a few days, it seemed untouched. Then, after about a week, Ghazala was straightening up and noticed a smattering of coins in the sack. The next day, there were more coins and less candy. This went on for a while, the nickels and dimes increasing, the Tootsie Rolls and Smarties dwindling. It wasn't hard to figure out that Humayun had been selling candy at school. The brilliant part was that he didn't rush in the day after

Halloween, when the other kids were still feeding off their own stashes — he waited a few days, until everyone else ran out but hadn't yet satisfied their sweet tooth. He had a captive, desperate market. Still, Ghazala put him out of business.

How many Halloweens would I have with my children? I'd already missed 1985's, missed all but the first two months of my youngest boy Omer's life. A year away to an adult is a long time, but to a child it's an eternity; days are weeks and weeks are months. I called a few times, on weekends, when I knew the boys would be home, but long distance was very expensive then, and I thought it better to send the money home. Once again we wrote often, Ghazala keeping me up-to-date on what was happening with the baby, with the older boys, with herself. When the gardenia she planted in the yard bloomed, she mailed me one of the first flowers. It had been flattened in transit, but the scent had not been pressed out. I could breathe it in and close my eyes and for a moment I'd be back in the yard, surrounded by my family.

The lady who managed the office raised an eyebrow at me, gave me a dubious stare. "What are you?" she asked. "Some kinda criminal?"

I laughed awkwardly. I was pretty sure she was joking. "No, no, nothing like that," I said, with what I hoped was enough sincerity just in case she wasn't.

"Let me get this straight. You just graduated from Harvard Law School, right?"

"Yes, ma'am. With a master's of law degree."

"And you want to work *here*?"

I didn't, really. I was in an office that reviewed mortgage documents for Fannie Mae and Freddie Mac, though its main appeal was that it was hiring immediately. It was located in Brighton, not far from the Commonwealth Avenue trolley, but the company had another office near Washington, where we planned to move. If I'd been interested in corporate or financial law, I would have chosen New York. But with my background and experience, I was a better fit for some kind of international law, which, happily, was also what I was most inclined toward. There would be more opportunities in the capital. In my daydreams, I wondered how we would decide whether to live by the Capitol or the White House.

"Well, I need a job right away," I said. "I'm going to move to Washington at some point, but right now my family is in Houston and I need to send them money and then I need to save money so we can move."

Probably more information than she needed, but I figured I should tell her the whole story.

"And you're sure you're not a criminal?" She smiled. Now I was sure she was joking.

I smiled, too. "No, not a criminal."

She seemed satisfied, and she seemed to like me. "Come back in the morning," she said. "Eight o'clock. We'll do the application then."

I'd already given up my apartment in Medford and rented the basement room in Allston, the next neighborhood over from Brighton. The commute was short, so the next morning I was at the office a few minutes before eight. I've always been punctual, a believer that getting things done early is better than rushing at the end.

The manager gave me an application, and after I'd completed it, she introduced me to my supervisor, a Filipino man named Leo. He led me down a long row of desks to the one all the way in the back. There was a computer on top and a box of files on the floor.

Leo spent the morning training me. The files were stuffed with mortgage documents — applications, HUD statements, lead paint disclosures, inspections, truth-in-lending declarations, ninety-six different forms in all — and the boxes were organized by state. My job was to go through each file, page by page, and make sure every form was included and complete. Then I would log it into the computer, stamp it as certified, and move on to the next one. If something was missing, I'd have to call the originator and get them to send it. If they complained or refused, I'd pass the file to Leo to deal with. Once I'd filled an entire box with certified files, the box would be sealed and shipped off to one of the quasigovernmental underwriters.

The job did not require a law degree from Punjab or Harvard or anywhere else. It was, to be honest, mind-numbing work, tedious, but not complicated. And there were a great many files, which meant I could work as much overtime as I wanted. After a couple of weeks, I had a job lined up with the Washington office as soon as I could get there. I'd given up on my White House–Capitol fantasy debate and started asking my coworkers where the best schools were. Montgomery County, Maryland, was the consensus choice. Ghazala and I decided we would settle in Silver Spring.

I returned every night to my rented basement room until, after about four weeks, the noise become unbearable. I wasn't getting enough rest. I paid the rent in advance each week, and one Friday decided I'd had enough. I kept my rent money, packed my suitcase, and found another room. It cost the same for a week, but the landlord also wanted a week's deposit up front. I didn't have it; I'd already sent every extra dollar to Ghazala. I could have written a check anyway, let it bounce, and repaid the landlord when I got paid the following week. That wouldn't have been stealing, exactly, just a slight delay I could play off as an innocent mistake.

But it wouldn't have been honest. I'd never written a bad check and wasn't about to start. I remembered my two rules for living in America: Pay my taxes and don't break any laws. Was bouncing a check a criminal offense? In certain circumstances, yes, maybe even these. But that didn't matter. In spirit if not in strict legal fact, it would have been wrong.

It was a Friday afternoon. I told the landlord I'd take the room but wanted to wait a week or so. My rental would start the following Monday, ten days off.

I went back to work, examined more mortgage files. In the late afternoon, my coworkers started logging off their computers, signing out for the weekend. Leo left close to six. By the time dusk brushed against the windows, I was the only one left. I thought about staying all night, imagined I'd get up early before anyone arrived, let everyone believe I'd just been eager to get started poring through dense paperwork. But what if I overslept? What if someone guessed I was homeless? What if someone found me there over the weekend, when the office was supposed to be closed? I didn't want pity or suspicion.

I stayed until darkness settled over the city, tucked my suitcase under my desk, and left. I wasn't sure where I would go, but the Public Garden seemed like my best option. It wasn't as big as the Common across Charles Street, but it was large enough to get purposely lost in, and leafier, too, more trees casting more dark shadows in which I could disappear. The garden was bordered by busy streets on all sides, but the trees and bushes muffled the noise. And Boston shut down early; the bars and restaurants closed up at two o'clock, the pedestrians and traffic would be all but gone thirty minutes later. It would be quiet then. If I could avoid the police, it wouldn't be a terrible place to get a few hours of rest.

At least it was summer.

The first night was long. I was being wary, keeping one eye open as long as possible, moving around probably more than I had to. Dawn was a relief. I made my way back to Brighton, found a McDonald's, went into the bathroom to wash up, spent a few dollars on a late, cheap breakfast, then wandered the city for the rest of the day, killing time.

The second night was easier, the surroundings more familiar. I started to discern hints of the police routine, foot patrols spaced about two hours apart between ten o'clock in the evening and two in the morning. I relaxed enough to slip my shoes off for a while.

Monday morning, I went to work early. I kept my coat buttoned over my wrinkled shirt.

By the third night, I'd figured out the rhythms of the park. I settled onto a bench, half-recumbent so I could pivot quickly upright. I would be out there only six more nights. Then I would have a proper room.

I adjusted myself on the bench, started making calculations in my head. In six weeks, I'd have saved enough to move to Maryland. Four weeks after that, if I stuck to my rent budget, I would have enough to fly to Houston, rent a U-Haul, hitch it to the back of the Chevy, and bring my family back with me. We would be moving forward, slowly, but together.

The police came and I sat up and then they went and I relaxed again.

I was thirty-six years old. I had worked on three continents. I had a beautiful family, I had a law license and a Harvard law degree.

I got up, walked past George Washington on his horse.

I was going to be an American citizen. We were all going to be Americans.

So sleeping in the park wasn't so bad, really, not when I put it in context. I closed one eye but kept the other half-open. The police wouldn't be back for two hours.

CHAPTER 8
SHINING CITY

There is a statue above the main entrance to the federal courthouse in Alexandria, Virginia, a bronze of Lady Justice. She is leaning forward, her feet anchored to the façade between two sandstone columns, blindfolded and holding a scale in each hand.

I glanced up at her as I pulled open the door, the statue a silhouette against the gray clouds rubbed into the springtime sky. That figure has always been, to me, a perfect representation of what is best about America, the idea that justice is blind to rich and poor, to Muslim and Christian, to black and white, that her scales will balance properly without regard to who stands before her. It has not always been executed with precision, but the ideal is exquisite, encapsulating the fundamental desire of people everywhere: to be treated with the same dignity as everyone else. In America, that ideal was written into law, and — before me — embodied in bronze.

I found my way to the designated courtroom. It had been three years since I'd taken my citizenship exam in Houston, but between studying and moving to Boston and then Maryland, it had taken a while for the bureaucracy to catch up with me. Finally, on April 29, 1988, I was going to swear an oath to the United States.

At the end of the summer of 1986, when New England was in its stickiest months, I'd transferred to the mortgage company's office in Maryland and found an apartment in a complex farther out, near what is now the Glenmont train yard, $400 a month for a two-bedroom unit on the ground floor so the boys would have a lawn to play on out back. After working for four weeks, I had enough extra money to fly to Houston and rent a U-Haul to drive to Silver Spring. We unpacked in the early autumn, which I remember because Ghazala enrolled the older boys in middle school the day after we moved in.

I didn't fully grasp it in the moment, but Silver Spring was an enormous relief for the boys, who — for the first time in their memory — didn't stand out. In Texas they'd been the light-brown kids with the unusual names in a sea of white Michaels and Jasons and Jennifers and Heathers. In Maryland, they were just another hue in a human rainbow of blacks and whites and Asians and Latinos. A child doesn't feel different, which no child wants to, when everyone else is different, too.

They were good kids. The older boys doted on Omer, our youngest son, who adored them, following his brothers like an eager puppy. If they were in their room, he'd plop himself outside the door and wait for them to realize he was there. They kept up with their studies, because that was still our number one rule. Though they were both athletic, we didn't allow them to play team sports at that age because we felt that would be too much of a distraction from their schoolwork. But they played a lot of basketball with their friends at a nearby playground and at home. Humayun liked to pretend he was Kareem Abdul-Jabbar, his favorite player and one of the greatest centers in NBA history, and he was constantly trying to perfect his own version of the skyhook.

We kept them on a short leash. Just as my grandparents hadn't wanted me to associate with certain kids, we didn't want our boys wandering the malls or hanging out unsupervised. There was nothing unique about our concerns, and we had no fears that one of our boys would tumble into, say, drugs or petty thievery. But adolescents have a preternatural ability to get in over their heads when left to their own devices, and we thought it best to keep them close for as long as we could do so practically without smothering them. So Ghazala always invited their friends to come to our apartment, where she could keep an eye on them. She'd bake cookies or make hamburgers and french fries, made sure our home was a place where adolescent boys would want to spend time.

We'd made a great life in America, I thought as I pushed open the door to the courtroom. In the front, just inside the rail that separates the spectators from the lawyers when court is in session, were a clerk and a pair of immigration officials standing behind a table with a pile of certificates stacked in the center. I gave them my name, and one of the officials flipped through the certificates until he found mine, which he placed facedown on one corner of the table.

Then I waited. I sat on a bench in the gallery with a few dozen other people, all races and colors, just as when I'd waited to take my exam. I wondered where they'd all come from, what circumstances pushed them or what yearning pulled them from the north and the south and the east and the west. Every immigrant has his reasons. Maybe they came to work or to escape persecution or to marry the person they loved. I knew even then that the details were only variations on a theme. Everyone who comes to America comes for the same basic reason: to be free to build a better life.

A bailiff stepped up to the bench. "All rise," he said, firm and clear. I stood and buttoned my coat while the judge, a silver-haired man, came out from his chambers and took his seat at the bench. He told us all to sit, and then gave a short speech welcoming us to the United States. We'd all been here for years — permanent residency is, after all, generally a prerequisite for citizenship — but now we would be official Americans. That was still a remarkable concept to me, one Ghazala and I had spoken of often with the boys. Where else, what other country, would allow strangers to join fully, regardless of their wealth or privilege or title? (We could have stayed in Dubai for three decades and been kicked out on a whim.) There was no requirement that anyone buy his citizenship; the huddled masses and wretched refuse were allowed in, too, to be embraced if they worked hard and followed the rules.

The judge asked us all to stand and raise our right hand, which he did as well. "Repeat after me," he said. "I hereby declare, on oath, that I absolutely and entirely renounce and abjure all allegiance and fidelity . . ."

He paused, waited for all of us to recite the phrase, the rolls and tangs of our accents harmonizing.

". . . to any foreign prince, potentate, state, or sovereignty . . ."

We echoed from the gallery.

". . . of whom or which I have heretofore been a subject or citizen . . ."

The words came out of my mouth automatically. In an instant, I was no longer Pakistani.

". . . that I will support and defend the Constitution and laws of the United States of America against all enemies, foreign and domestic . . ."

And in the next instant, I was swearing allegiance to a new nation. I continued to recite by reflex, following instructions, careful not to forget or fumble the next phrase. But I was also fully aware of the weight of that text. People who are American by birth

— my youngest son, for example — are never required to make such an explicit promise in order to be granted the full protections of the Constitution. But I was saying, in those twenty-two words, that I would hold that document, the *promise* of that ancient parchment, supreme. It is not difficult to passively support a framework of governance, but we all repeated, consciously and deliberately, a precise and important word: We would *defend* the Constitution, which is altogether more solemn than simply cheerleading.

The judge finished the rest of the oath in fragments we could repeat: "that I will bear true faith and allegiance to the same; that I will bear arms on behalf of the United States when required by the law; that I will perform noncombatant service in the Armed Forces of the United States when required by the law; that I will perform work of national importance under civilian direction when required by the law. . . ." We recited each of those pledges, our right hands still held aloft, and then the judge read the final clause: "and that I take this obligation freely, without any mental reservation or purpose of evasion; so help me God."

I meant every word of it.

"Congratulations," the judge said, and motioned for us to be seated. "Listen for your name to be called, and then come forward."

The clerk picked up the certificate on the top of the stack, read a name, and handed the document to the judge, who in turn gave it to the smiling Latina woman who stepped up to receive it. The clerk proceeded through the pile. When she got to Khan, I walked forward, shook the judge's hand, and returned to the gallery. I held the paper gently, careful not to crease or dimple it. It was beautiful, a page of ornate and looping text, my personal details typed into underlined gaps. My picture of me, unsmiling behind big glasses, a bow tie knotted at my neck, was on the left side, the bottom of it crimped by an embossed circular seal. Across the top, flanking a gold eagle clutching an olive branch in one set of talons, arrows in the other, were blocky, shadowed letters that read CERTIFICATE OF NATURALIZATION.

I was a citizen. I was an American.

I was mesmerized by the certificate, by what it represented. Looking back, I'm not entirely sure how I felt. Relieved. Euphoric. Patriotic. I suppose all of those emotions alchemized into a slightly numbing concoction. I'd felt like an American for years by then, but the knowledge always was there, gnawing almost imperceptibly in the back of my mind, that it wasn't yet official. Now I'd been validated.

The judge dismissed us. In the hallway, there was a table with voter registration forms and miniature American flags. I picked up one of each, then gave the flag a playful wave and carried it outside, beneath the statue of Lady Justice and into the gray of the overcast afternoon, which to me suddenly seemed gloriously clear and bright.

As a practical matter, our lives did not change. There is no trophy for becoming a citizen. No one gives you a promotion or a bonus check. I didn't even get called for jury duty. Instead, I got up Monday morning and rode the Metro to work, the same as I had before I was a citizen, the same as I would every day after. The situation reminded me of the Zen maxim: *Before enlightenment, chop wood, carry water. After enlightenment, chop wood, carry water.*

I didn't enjoy the work at the mortgage firm, but I was good at it. I was a supervisor by then, doing the same job Leo, my Filipino friend in Boston, did: training new hires, reviewing everyone else's work, and, if there was a problem with a recalcitrant loan originator, working it out over the phone. I was overqualified, but there are a lot of overqualified people doing a lot of jobs. What mattered was the paycheck, supporting my family, making my own way in America.

Summer came and went, then autumn. We saved enough to replace the Impala, which was then seventeen years old, with a used minivan, the quintessential American family vehicle. I wasn't unhappy, but that was irrelevant, because happiness wasn't my concern. In fact, I'd consciously excised "being happy" from my immediate goals. What I wanted then, more than anything else, was a peaceful life, one free of conflict, with no clashing in the streets, no crises of conscience. That might seem a modest ambition, unless you've come from a place where a peaceful life is a luxury. Contentment is too often underrated.

One evening the following January, I sat down on the couch in the living room of our small apartment and clicked on the television, which was on a little table in front of me. Ronald Reagan was on all the networks. He was making a speech, his farewell address after eight years in office. I liked Reagan. I could mark my time in

America by his time in office: I saw him speak in Houston, not long after I arrived and when he was still a candidate for president, in an amphitheater carved into a park. Everyone else in the throng wore T-shirts in the Texas heat, but I thought I should dress appropriately, so I stood at the top of the hill in my suit and tie, the best-dressed person there. Imagine, I thought as I walked down Richmond Avenue from the park afterward, an ordinary man can be in the audience for someone who might be president. In Pakistan, such a privilege might trickle down to the cousin of a governor. In Texas, anyone could just show up and be part of democracy; no one asked who I was, demanded my identification, inquired as to my residency status. Reagan spoke that day, as he often did, about the greatness of America, about what it could still become. He was full of a candidate's optimism, which is what an immigrant wants to believe, *does* believe, about his own future. I walked home in the dusk, thinking that I would vote for Reagan if I were a citizen.

I became a citizen too late to vote for Reagan. Nine years had gone by.

Now it was January 11, 1989. I was alone in the living room. The older boys were in the small bedroom, either finishing their homework or already in bed, and Ghazala was with Omer in the master bedroom. He still slept with his mother, and I slept in the den, surrounded by boxes of books we'd never gotten around to unpacking.

The couch, brown and worn and matching the loveseat set next to it at an angle, was squishy where the springs had gone soft. I didn't mind. It was comfortable enough.

I listened intently as President Reagan — my president — said goodbye to the country. It was as eloquent a speech as he'd ever given, still laced with the optimism I'd heard years earlier, as if eight long years in arguably the most demanding job on the planet hadn't tarnished his underlying faith in the goodness of America. For more than eighteen minutes, he reminisced about his time in office, about what he'd accomplished, what the nation could still accomplish.

"And that's about all I have to say tonight, except for one thing," Reagan said. "These past few days when I've been at that window upstairs, I've thought a bit of the 'shining city upon a hill.' "

I leaned forward, rested my elbows on my knees.

"The phrase comes from John Winthrop," he said, "who wrote it to describe the America he imagined. What he imagined was important because he was an early Pilgrim, an early freedom man. He journeyed here on what today we'd call a little wooden boat. And like the other Pilgrims, he was looking for a home that would be free."

My eyes locked onto the screen. It was as if the president was speaking directly to me.

"I've spoken of the shining city all my political life, but I don't know if I ever quite communicated what I saw when I said it. But in my mind it was a tall, proud city built on rocks stronger than the oceans, windswept, God-blessed, and teeming with people of all kinds living in harmony and peace, a city with free ports that hummed with commerce and creativity. And if there had to be city walls, the walls had doors and the doors were open to anyone with the will and the heart to get here. That's how I saw it, and see it still."

What a beautiful city. Such a beautiful vision.

There was a muffled thump from the boys' room, nothing more than a child turning over, dropping a book. But I turned my head quickly, instinctively. In one short swivel, I could take in the whole sweep of our apartment. Tiny kitchen with an electric range, simple wooden dining table behind the couch, four windows that looked out over grass and, beyond, trees. It seemed to me one of the more humble dwellings in that shining city.

A relative of Ghazala's had asked me once why I would want to stay in America. "Come back home," he'd said. "There, you are just an ordinary person. Here, you will be someone." And it was true, I would be Someone in Pakistan. At this point in my career, fifteen years after getting my law license, I would probably be practicing in the High Court. I would have homes in Lahore and Islamabad, fine cars, a servant hired to clean and another to cook.

But at what cost? How many times would I have turned my head, looked the other way?

One of my brothers and his children had come to visit us in Maryland about a year after we moved there. Our boys took them to the park to play basketball, or tried to: Their uncle saw a park police station and immediately stopped, turned around, walked in the other direction, and insisted that all the boys come with him. Of course he did, because that was the reality he knew.

In Pakistan, the police were to be avoided, and if you couldn't avoid them, they were to be bribed. His sons teased Humayun because he didn't know the proper way to offer a bribe, how to fold a hundred-rupee note into a tight square, hold it between your thumb and forefinger with just the corner peeking out so the cop would see it when you offered your hand and wished him a good evening.

It would never occur to my American boys to bribe a police officer.

"And how stands the city on this winter night?" Reagan asked. I turned back to the television. "More prosperous, more secure, and happier than it was eight years ago. But more than that: After two hundred years, two centuries, she still stands strong and true on the granite ridge, and her glow has held steady no matter what storm. And she's still a beacon, still a magnet for all who must have freedom, for all the pilgrims from all the lost places who are hurtling through the darkness, toward home."

One night when I was a boy, watching the moon from my cot, my grandfather came and stood over me. "I have a question for you," he said. He motioned for me to move my feet to one side, then sat at the end of the bed, fixed his gaze on me.

"Where do you think," he asked, "you can go to find God?"

I considered his query for a moment, wondering if there was a correct answer, something I'd missed in my studies. I could tell from his face, though, through the gentleness of his expression, that he wasn't quizzing me but rather teaching.

"I don't know," I said.

"Well, some people go into the forests to find God," he said. "But if he was there, the sheep and the cows and the animals of the forest already would have found him." A pause. "Some people go to the river and onto the ocean to find God. But if he were there, wouldn't the fish and the frogs have already found him?" Another pause. "And some people go into the mountains, but if he was there, the mountaineers and the goats already would have found him."

A longer pause, my grandfather looking at me with a kind of half smile.

"So where do you go to find God?"

He smiled widely now. "Ah, that is for you to tell me."

I went to sleep that night turning the puzzle over in my head. In my child's mind, the mountains made the most sense, since God was up in Heaven and mountains were tall and closer to Heaven. Or maybe in the forest, because God created the trees and the pastures and all the creatures of the earth, and he might want to be with them, out in nature. But he created the oceans, too, and there were a lot of creatures beneath the seas and a lot of Heaven spread out above them. Maybe that was where to find him.

The next night, my grandfather told me a different story, and then said good night.

"Wait," I said. "You never told me where to find God."

He smiled and nodded. "Later," he said. "Keep thinking."

I thought for another day and another night and then the following day, too, and still I wasn't sure. On the third night, I asked him again.

"You don't know?" he said. "That's all right. So many people don't know." He shook his head slowly. "God is in the hearts of people," he told me. "And that is where you find him, out among the people."

I must have been eight or nine years old then, and I distilled the theology of that lesson to its literal core: that God could be disguised as anyone in a crowd, a pauper or a shopkeeper or the man with the red and green flags guarding the railroad crossing,

251

and that I therefore should treat everyone with respect, just in case. As I grew older, though, I understood what my grandfather intended with that lesson: It was a guide to living a just and merciful life. If God had created everyone and everything, then he also had instilled into each person a holy dignity. Yet the result, whether I considered it literally or metaphorically, was the same. Every person, no matter his or her station, is to be accorded the respect inherent in his or her creation.

My own children had heard a version of that story more times than I could count. I thought of it often on Sunday mornings, when Ghazala was in the kitchen, steaming pots of rice and boiling red beans. She would also prepare a protein of some kind, chicken or beef we bought in bulk. The older boys and I would form an assembly line, scooping a portion of each — rice, beans, protein — into Styrofoam containers. We would box up dozens of meals, at least fifty, sometimes a hundred, load them into the minivan, and then drive into Washington, to the streets and parks where homeless people huddled.

"The people in shelters, they have access to food," I told the boys the first time we crossed the bridge into the city. "But some people don't want to go to the shelters or can't go, for whatever reason. But the reason doesn't matter — they deserve a hot meal, too."

I never talked about what those reasons might be. Who were we to judge? Being hungry isn't a moral failing — it's an empty stomach. If we could share, if we could fill a person's belly for at least a little while, we were required by faith and human decency to do so.

I never told them I was once so hungry I ate discarded bread.

I pulled to the curb. Four unwashed and disheveled men had arranged blankets on the sidewalk, a desperate little campsite. I turned to the boys sitting behind me. "You can start here," I said. "But don't just walk up and give them a meal. Ask them first. Say, 'Hello, would you like something to eat?' "

Humayun was twelve years old, his brother thirteen. They stared at me with mild confusion, perhaps a touch of anxiety.

"These are people," I said. "They're not animals you're feeding at the zoo. Treat them like people. If they say yes, then talk to them, and don't just stand over them. If they're sitting down, you sit down, too. Just treat them the way you'd like to be treated.

They might not remember what they ate, but they'll remember that someone spoke to them."

Both boys nodded. They were old enough to understand. They each picked up Styrofoam cartons and got out of the van. I rolled forward a few yards, far enough that I didn't look like a sentry, but not so far that Ghazala and I couldn't keep an eye on them. We believed in dignity, but we weren't naïve. We watched as the boys approached, their body language betraying their nervousness. We couldn't hear, but we saw the men smile, and then the boys squat down, eye level, and hand each a box. They stayed there only a few minutes, then hurried back to the van. "Where next?" Humayun asked. He was beaming.

We did that every Sunday for years. As the boys got older, their friends joined us. When they were in high school, we'd distribute all of our meals and then drop Humayun and Shaharyar at one of the shelters in the city, where they would tutor people in reading and math and computer skills.

This was never an exercise in smug altruism, a pious *noblesse oblige* that the boys could later craft into essays for their college applications. We were instilling in them, or hoped we were, a sense of community even among strangers, a belief that we each have a fundamental duty to others, to share what we can and help where possible. That was how we lived.

One morning in 1993, I saw a woman with a headscarf fast-walking down a street in Washington, almost running, her arms pulled in close, hugging her waist, as if she was trying to make herself as small as possible. I pulled to the curb, rolled down the passenger-side window, leaned over. "Is everything okay?" I said.

She snapped her head toward me but didn't break stride. "No English, no English," she said.

She was clearly distressed. I stopped the car, put on my hazard lights, got out and hurried after her. When I caught up, she stopped and said something in Arabic, a language I could understand and speak clumsily. I managed to figure out that she was from Morocco and had been hired by foreign diplomats as household help, but that she'd been kept in virtual slavery. She was escaping.

Her passport had been taken by her employers. She had no identification and no money. What could I do? Leave her to the streets? Let her fend for herself, not speaking English, not knowing where to go, whom to trust?

"He helped a woman and children in need," the Prophet, peace be upon him, said of the pious man after the last hajj. "He sacrificed and shared what he had. This — this! — is what I have been teaching you for twenty-three years."

I took her home. Her name was Haddeh and she lived in our basement, a comfortably finished space, for three years. Once she was settled, she found work with another family, people who treated her fairly, respectfully. Friends of friends, meanwhile, heard what we'd done for Haddeh and asked us to help a Hindu woman named Pushpa, who'd found herself in a similar situation. So Pushpa lived with us for a while, too, which was awkward only when the boys woke up one morning to loud voices from the basement: Pushpa's Hindu shrine was somehow interfering with Haddeh's prayers, and for a brief while we had a faith-off in the basement. She stayed only a few months, until the Hindu temple helped her find another employer to sponsor her visa.

There also was a student struggling to get through Howard University who stayed with us for a few months, and finally there was Mr. Elgin. He was a homeless veteran I would see most mornings when I came off the Theodore Roosevelt Bridge onto Constitution Avenue. On my drive to work, I would give him a few dollars if I was stopped in traffic, but I realized that that wasn't doing more than getting him through another day and night on the streets. I finally asked him if there was something more I could offer, maybe help get him set up in an apartment.

"No," he said. "I'm too sick and couldn't handle an apartment on my own." He looked at me with rheumy eyes, suddenly wet with tears. "But I don't want to die homeless."

So I took him home, too. Haddeh had moved back to Morocco and married a man named Khan (which I'm sure was just a coincidence, but that fact still makes me smile), so the basement was open. Mr. Elgin, incontinent, his health rapidly deteriorating, stayed with us for a few months, heating his meals in a microwave we bought, Ghazala cleaning up after him. We moved him to a hospice for the last days of his life, where he died cared for and peacefully.

Was it dangerous, sending our children into the streets, bringing strangers into our home? A little, maybe. But we were careful. And sometimes, doing the right thing requires some element of risk. Which was more important — teaching our children to help people, or teaching them to be afraid? And which was more important to Haddeh, to Mr. Elgin?

"When you go to an orchard," I asked the boys once, by way of explanation, "and you see a person picking fruit, is he the one who planted the trees?" They looked at me blankly, not sure of the answer, just as I wasn't when my grandfather asked me such questions. "No, probably not," I said, getting to the point. "He is harvesting what others have planted." I let that settle in for a beat. "Each of you," I said, "is a gardener."

I had come from a country with few such gardeners. Though I was blessed to have my grandparents and parents, in Pakistan at that time, one's place in the world at birth was a reliable indicator of where one's place would be when he died. Those born poor remained poor, the rich remained rich, quite often by preying on the poor, and everyone in the middle struggled just to stay there. The fundamental problem wasn't autocracy or Islamization, but primal exploitation.

And yet I had made it to America in part because others held to that belief in community, because caring individuals had shared what they could. A tea seller fed me on credit; Sheikh Imtiaz had risked his reputation, and no small amount of cash, to allow a desperate student to take his exams; a cabbie in Dubai and a sardar ji in Houston had given shelter to a stranger; Paulette, a woman I'd never met, brought food for hungry children. Where would I have been without each of those people, in fact, without *all* of those people?

At the same time, though, I was not consciously repaying a debt to any of them. Ghazala and I and our children, I would like to believe, would have tried to help others even if I'd had the money to pay for my exams, for hotel rooms in Dubai and Houston, even if I had never crossed paths with any of those kind souls. My grandfather told me I would find God among the people, and I still believed in his wisdom.

The phone on my desk rang with a sharp chirp one afternoon in 1990. I answered, and a woman, her voice unfamiliar, introduced herself.

"My name is Ellen," she said, "and I'm helping a law firm try to fill a position you might be interested in. Do you have a few minutes to talk?"

A quick jolt of adrenaline shot through me. I'd been weary of mortgages since my second day in Boston, but I was living paycheck to paycheck, working overtime to make ends meet, without ever the free week or month or however long it would take to find a job more appropriate to my credentials. I'd simply never had the time to invest in looking for another job. Now this woman, Ellen, was calling, unsolicited and out of the blue.

"Yes," I said immediately. "Of course I have time."

Ellen didn't tell me the name of the law firm, only that it was a large one involved in a complex case that involved an enormous number of documents that needed to be organized and managed. Then she told me the salary, which was more than twice what I was earning.

"Do you think you might be interested?" she asked.

I was already writing my résumé in my head. "Yes, very," I said.

This, we've all been told and I still believed, was how things were supposed to happen in America. Work hard, follow the rules, and opportunities will present themselves. Being lucky didn't hurt; having years of experience wrestling with reams and reams of dense paperwork at the exact moment that a law firm needed someone with those exact qualifications might be serendipity, or maybe karma. But if part of success is being in the right place at the right time, a person still had to put himself there.

I typed up my résumé that night, got it to Ellen, and a few days later took time off from work to meet with one of the partners, a man named Mark. I didn't recognize the name of the law firm at the time, but learned later it was one of the premier litigation outfits in the country. And the case it was hiring for was indeed complex, involving two large corporations with thousands of individual sets of facts to be litigated. My job would be to organize the case documents — all of the discovery and related files.

"We need you to read each of these files," Mark told me. "Twice, front to back, because the answer is always in the fine print."

I smiled. I heard an echo from my apprenticeship in Pakistan, when I was taught to read the FIRs like a movie script. *A defense is almost always hiding in the gaps.* "This is what I do now," I told Mark. "I read paper."

I was hired. It was exciting work, odd as that might sound, poring through those documents; I felt like a detective solving multiple puzzles. The hours were long, from early in the morning until late in the evening, sometimes six, seven days a week.

The extra money I was earning allowed us to move out of the apartment and into a three-bedroom house on Layhill Road, a few blocks from John F. Kennedy High School, where Shaharyar was a freshman and Humayun would follow in the fall. We splurged on a real basketball hoop for the boys, so they could stop throwing the ball at a chalk square they'd draw on the back wall and then redraw every time the rain washed it away, and I bought myself a Toyota Camry for the commute into D.C. Other than that, we continued to live modestly, as that was both our nature and, by then, a habit.

Three years later, while the litigation continued to plod along at the usual pace of such complicated cases, another headhunter called. She had an offer I might be interested in, at a larger firm that was looking for someone to develop and manage its electronic discovery department. Personal computers by then had been ubiquitous for more than a decade, and paper records that used to be stored in warehoused boxes were instead filed digitally. On the one hand, the switch to electronic records was a revolution in convenience and efficiency. On the other, tremendous volumes of emails and contracts and reports and such that might be relevant to a lawsuit were coded onto hard drives and servers; accessing the proper material wasn't as simple as copying files onto a fresh drive. Caches of records need to be sorted and cataloged, documents need to be recoded into a usable form, and metadata must be preserved. To use the simplest example, if you copy a year's worth of emails into a single file, it will appear that those emails were all written on the same day — a point any competent lawyer would seize on. Were they edited? Are they even legitimate?

That was fascinating, cutting-edge work, at a firm with a global reach. Plus, the money was better. I jumped at the chance.

The change, as changes so often do, inspired a moment of reflection: Twenty years earlier, I'd stood at Sheikh Imtiaz's door, panicked that I wouldn't be able to take my exams and thus get a license to practice in Pakistan. Fifteen years earlier, I'd taught English to immigrants by day and watched over an office lobby all night, saving every penny. Less than eight years earlier, I was so stretched for cash that I slept on a bench in a park.

But I'd played by the rules. I'd worked

hard, I'd taken care of my family, I'd sworn an oath to defend the Constitution of the United States, a document I'd revered since I'd read it so many years before. And, finally, I'd realized my version of the American Dream. My wife and children were American citizens — our youngest son by birth, Ghazala and the older boys since they were naturalized in 1991. We would never live flamboyantly, but we were comfortable, no longer worried about accounting for every penny every week. Our oldest son was about to graduate as the valedictorian of his high school class. His brother, a year behind, was an excellent student as well, and he'd taken up sprinting for the track team and swimming competitively. Neither of them, nor Omer, had ever given us any trouble.

Wait: That's not entirely true. One time, a boy in the high school cafeteria made fun of Humayun for fasting during Ramadan, and Shaharyar slapped him for it. That got Ghazala a call from the principal. And Humayun did sneak out one evening after he was supposed to be in bed. He didn't go far, just across Layhill to play basketball on the lighted courts, and didn't stay out very late, but Ghazala locked all the doors and windows so he would have to knock to get back in, which made the episode as farcical as it was disobedient.

Even in the worst light, it's hard to see either of those as a major transgression. In the best, how could we criticize defending a brother, even if slapping wasn't perhaps the best way to do so? Of course, there may have been other wrongdoings that Ghazala and I never discovered. But even so, it was plain to see that they were good, smart, popular, and dignified boys who seemed to have absorbed the fundamental values we'd tried to instill. When I noticed with mild annoyance, for instance, that Humayun was spending an inordinate amount of time at the pool, I asked him why. He told me he was teaching disabled children to swim.

"But when do you have time to practice?" I asked.

"I make time," he said. "When you see their faces . . . I mean, I can't *not* do it."

Isn't that what we'd taught our boys? To be good citizens? Yes, it was. That they'd learned so well meant only that we'd been blessed.

CHAPTER 9
BABA

"I want to join ROTC," Humayun said.

Ghazala set her cup down on the wooden table. "Okay," she said. "Very good. And what is that?"

"It stands for Reserve Officers' Training Corps. For the Army."

Ghazala's eyes widened, as did mine. "You want to join the Army?" she asked, a trace of maternal alarm in her voice.

"Yes," he said, firm and confident. "Not right now. I mean, ROTC is here, so I'll finish college, but after that I'd be an officer in the Army."

It was a glorious spring morning in 1997, and we were sitting in the sun outside Alderman Library on the campus of the University of Virginia. We'd been coming to Charlottesville several times a month for more than two years, since Shaharyar enrolled the autumn after he graduated high school. He'd been accepted as a Jefferson

266

Scholar, the university's most prestigious honor, a four-year, merit-based scholarship, including tuition, room and board, and a stipend for living expenses.

Humayun initially chose to enroll at the University of Maryland for a year, but it seemed inevitable, in hindsight, that he would follow Shaharyar to UVA. "Irish twins," they used to joke, inseparable since they were babies in Dubai. Humayun spent many weekends visiting his brother, made friends on his brother's campus, got comfortable in Charlottesville, and decided to start over as a freshman in the fall of 1996. When he was accepted, it was Shaharyar who called me at the office, bursting with pride. "My brother got into UVA," he told me. I remember being struck by that phrasing — *my brother,* in the same way I would say *my son,* reflecting and amplifying the glow of his success. Ghazala and I and Omer moved to Virginia then, too: Humayun was paying tuition, which was far less expensive for Virginia residents than for out-of-state students. Plus, our townhouse in Centreville was also almost two hours closer to Charlottesville than Silver Spring was, so it was easier to visit. There was no Starbucks then, but there was a fine coffee shop in Alderman Library. We'd stop there often with one or both boys, get a drink, and find someplace quiet to sit, which is what we'd done that morning.

"Oh, no," Ghazala said. "You can't join the Army. There are so many wars going on. You could get hurt. You could get killed!" She winced, as if she'd pierced her heart just by saying those words aloud.

Humayun leveled his gaze at his mother. He had brown eyes, clear and kind and knowing beyond his years, and my stoic mouth. But we could still see the boy he'd been not so long ago in the smoothness of his cheeks, the generosity of his hairline, the dimple in his chin. "Umie," he said patiently, "the United States isn't fighting any wars right now. And even if it was, people die on the street every day." That was indisputably true: A friend of the family, a boy about Humayun's age, had lost control of his motorcycle on a curve on Interstate 66, skidded, tumbled, and died before the ambulance got him to the hospital. "If people die," Humayun said, "it's just destiny."

Ghazala did not appear comforted by that bit of fatalism. Let destiny take some other mother's son.

"Besides," Humayun said, "the Army isn't just about fighting wars, and ROTC is here on campus. It's about honor and discipline and respect, too." That also was indisputably true. We'd seen cadets in their fatigues and tan boots, walking the campus with a quiet confidence. An obvious sense of purpose seemed to radiate from them. They looked you in the eye when they passed, and said "Good morning, sir" or "Good evening, ma'am."

"And I like the cadets," Humayun said. He looked off into the middle distance, focused more on his thoughts than anything he could see. "I don't know," he said. "But when I'm around them, I just feel like I'm in my element."

I could understand that. Humayun had always been an ordered, disciplined child, not difficult, but particular. When he was a toddler, he would refuse to put on his shoes until his socks were perfectly aligned, fussing until his heel and toes settled into their proper spots, no wrinkles or bulges in the fabric. He was tidy and efficient as a child, his toys and books always put away where they belonged, his schoolwork always finished early, and he preferred his hair clipped military short. "Look at him, always getting things done," Ghazala would say. "He's like a little Army soldier." To her, that was a compliment: She was fourteen years old

269

when Pakistan went to war with India in 1965, and she remembered the soldiers through the soft filter of a teenaged girl — as noble patriots, handsome in their crisp khaki uniforms.

Was that ironic, that her son would want to be one of those patriots, handsome in his own uniform? Maternal instinct has a way of bringing the adolescent girl's gauzy memory into focus.

Humayun wasn't a gung-ho warrior, though. He had never played soldier as a boy, never talked, as some boys do, of becoming a Navy SEAL or a Green Beret. He was, however, instinctively protective — quick to stand up for other kids who were bullied. In middle school, he had a Trinidadian friend, an overweight kid whom others used to call Fatrick, a cruel play on his middle name, Patrick. Humayun would walk the halls with him like a bodyguard, and he'd push kids away when they taunted and punched at Patrick. Still, he wasn't aggressive. He was calm, philosophical, more interested in how people thought, what made them tick, than in dominating anyone.

The morning sun was warm on the back of my neck. I hadn't said anything yet, just listened to Humayun and his mother.

A snippet of a song played in my head,

the lyrics and the melody tripping across my synapses. I'd asked him once, not so long before that morning, what kind of music he listened to. "A lot of different things," he said. "I'll burn you a CD." When he gave it to me, he told me his favorite song was the one by Sting, "Shape of My Heart." Looking at Humayun, I could hear the chorus:

I know that the spades are the swords of a soldier

I know that the clubs are weapons of war

I know that diamonds mean money for this art

But that's not the shape of my heart.

I knew my son's heart. Whatever drew my tender psychology major to ROTC, it wasn't a thirst for war. No one understands the ugliness of war more intimately than a soldier, or views it more warily than a young student training to be an officer.

But I had my own concerns. Finally, I spoke.

"What does this mean," I asked, "for your future?" I had seen the army in Pakistan, and not through Ghazala's girlhood eyes. A soldier there was a soldier for life. He was subsumed by an immense organization, absorbed into it until he became no more than a tiny cog in a giant machine. This was a lifelong occupation, and it could change a person. I didn't want the military to take Humayun forever.

"Well, I'd be commissioned as a lieutenant when I graduate," he said. "I'd do four years, and then I thought I'd go to law school like I'd planned, except the Army would help pay for it."

I nodded slowly. I'd always pushed the boys to get degrees beyond their bachelor's, told them to read more, learn how to write well. *A person is not complete until his education is complete.* "I have a degree from Harvard," I used to tease them. "I know a thing or two about this." But raising children, I thought, sitting there on the UVA campus, was like planting trees. You can tend them, nurture them, but they set their own roots, their branches reaching toward whatever sun they choose to follow, until one day they leaf and flower on their own. And then we can only stand back and admire what has grown, and pray that the soil beneath them is firm.

"You've really thought this through, haven't you?"

"I have," Humayun said. "It's what I want to do."

We sat in silence for a moment. Humayun clearly wanted our approval, but I suspected he would be only disappointed, not dissuaded, without it. And how could we say no? Despite Ghazala's fears and my concerns, we knew he would be an exemplary cadet, and a fine officer.

The hardest part of being a parent is letting go.

"Very well, then," I said. "When would you start?"

Humayun smiled. There might have been a hint of relief on his face, but I'm still not sure. "In the fall, Baba." The boys always called me Baba. "I'll start in the fall."

The four men galumphing down the stairs with our furniture, dinging the walls and stumbling over their own feet, were not professional movers. I'd hired them that morning from a day labor pool, right after I'd picked up the U-Haul, to help empty our townhouse in Centreville, load the truck, and unload it again in Bristow, Virginia. We'd decided to move to a house a little closer to Charlottesville, and we thought we would save some money hiring out the heavy lifting and doing the rest ourselves.

An hour into the packing, it was not going well. The men I'd hired were a disheveled and disorganized lot, accustomed to manual labor but not at all practiced in the choreography of efficient loading, of what to carry in what order. They were grabbing the nearest box or table or bed and careening out the door, shoving some of it into the truck, depositing the rest on the lawn to figure out later. I did my best to guide them, but I wasn't a mover either. Mostly, I barked worried orders — "Be careful with that! Watch the wall!" — that seemed neither helpful nor effective.

I heard a car pull up in front of the house. Shaharyar driving, Humayun in the passenger seat. They got out, came toward the door. Humayun could tell from the look on my face and the sound of my voice that I was frustrated.

"How you doing, Baba?" He had a bemused smile, as if he was watching a mildly and unnecessarily chaotic comedy sketch.

"Well, I'm just . . ." I didn't quite know what to say.

He put his hand on my shoulder. "It's all right. Let me handle this." Humayun turned toward the day laborers skittering around the townhouse. "Hey, guys," he said, loud but friendly. "C'mon with me a minute." He swept his arm up in a loose wave, a signal that they should follow him outside.

I stayed near the front door as four men

shuffled after Humayun. He gathered them at the back of the truck, and they stood in a loose arc in front of him. Humayun's back was to me, and he was far enough away that I couldn't hear what he was saying. But he seemed calm, gesturing with his hands deliberately, rather than as if he was on an authoritarian rant. And the men didn't seem intimidated or even annoyed; they were attentive, cooperative, nodding approval.

Then they got back to work. But it was as if Humayun had fired the old, stumbling crew and hired four new men. They walked quickly back to the house, and almost in a single-file line, turned toward the dining room, studied the boxes and furniture for a moment, appraising the situation. They each picked up a chair, carried it outside, set it near the truck, came back inside. Two men grabbed the last two chairs, and the other two positioned themselves at opposite ends of the table, lifted it, and moved toward the door — carefully this time, watching the walls.

That went on for more than an hour. I didn't know what Humayun had said to them, but whatever it was, he'd transformed four unskilled laborers into a cohesive unit. At the risk of making too obvious an analogy, it was almost as if they were a well-trained squad.

This struck me at first as remarkable. But as I watched the men carrying our possessions out of the house, tightly packing the truck, it occurred to me that it also was entirely predictable. Ghazala and I could see the effect ROTC was having on Humayun, the shift in his demeanor and bearing.

It had been months since I'd dropped Humayun in a parking lot on the west side of the UVA campus, in August 1997, where he got on a bus with the other ROTC cadets for a week of orientation at Fort A. P. Hill, a training facility near Bowling Green, Virginia. When the UVA semester began, he had one class a week of military science, a morning or two of physical training — running and calisthenics and the like — and, on Tuesday afternoons, three hours of what was called lab. He learned how to stand in formation and march and handle weapons, all the basics of soldiering, but the focus was on leadership strategies, how to organize a scattering of trainees into a cohesive unit. That he could use those same skills to arrange four strangers into an effective moving team wasn't, in retrospect, surprising. Before my eyes, he was morphing into a leader. It was amazing.

ROTC hadn't changed him so much as it had amplified traits he'd always possessed, his sense of order and discipline. He was living in a single room in Hereford College, a collection of dormitories and common areas near the UVA stadium. As part of securing a room there, he'd written an essay that focused on the university's legacy of public service and, fittingly, its founder, Thomas Jefferson. Humayun had long been a student of Jefferson, as had I. When the boys were little, I used to take them to the gleaming white Jefferson Memorial at the edge of the Tidal Basin. Under the dome, we would read the inscriptions carved into the walls — the paragraph of self-evident truths from the Declaration of Independence, the four sentences from a religious freedom bill Jefferson drafted in 1777, the excerpt from a letter he wrote in 1816 ("Institutions must advance also, and keep pace with the times. We might as well require a man to wear still the coat which fitted him when a boy, as civilized society to remain ever under the regimen of their barbarous ancestors"). In his essay, Humayun distilled those Jeffersonian lessons to their essence. "Liberty requires vigilance and sacrifice," he wrote. "The beneficiaries of liberty must always bear this in mind, and keep it safe from attacks."

He kept his room immaculate. The first time we visited, I was examining the books lined neatly on his shelves, the spines all even with one another, a perfect, flat wall of bindings. I noticed that at one corner, on a shelf at eye level, he'd stacked white buttons of various sizes next to a spool of white thread, the loose end of which slipped through the eye of a needle. I moved along the shelf, and at the opposite corner, also at eye level, there was a collection of black buttons next to a needle attached to a spool of black thread.

"Humayun," I said, "why do you have these buttons here? And the thread?"

"Huh?" He looked up from his desk. "Oh, those. It's just easier that way. You know, if I'm in a hurry and a button's loose, it's easier just to have them ready."

"I see," I said. "I suppose that makes sense." Which it did, except I never would have thought to keep a loaded needle on my bedroom shelf.

"And why do you keep all your clothes under the bed?" Ghazala asked. She pulled two plastic bins from beneath the frame, popped off the lids. Both were full of shirts and pants and underwear, everything crisply folded.

"Some of those are dirty," he said. "The ones on the left. Those are dirty."

"You fold your dirty clothes?" I said.

"Yeah. They take up less space that way."

I nodded. That also made sense, but, again, it had never occurred to me to fold my laundry before I washed it.

Out of context, those might seem like neurotic habits, the obsessive threading and folding of a young man suffering a compulsion toward unreasonable neatness. Yet there was no hint of that. Humayun, in fact, was quite easygoing, affable and relaxed with a sly, dry sense of humor. When he was crafting something funny in his mind, he'd get this look, a sort of half smirk combined with a slow nod, as if he was winking with his whole head; a friend once said it was like an actor breaking character, letting you in on the joke. None of that had changed. He was still the Humayun we'd always known. He'd just figured out more efficient ways to maximize his time and space, to make the best use of the resources at hand. I was impressed.

Those were my thoughts as I watched our household goods being packed into a truck. It all made sense: Humayun, groomed for military leadership, had organized a small squad of privates for a mission. He hadn't yelled at anyone or issued threats. He just spoke quietly, apparently choosing the right words to maximize the resources at hand.

The unloading at our new home in Bristow was just as efficient, maybe more so, the four laborers now practiced, operating as a fine-tuned machine. When the U-Haul was empty, the furniture and the boxes all lugged to their appropriate rooms, I pulled Humayun aside.

"Thank you," I said. "I'm very impressed with what you did, how you got them working together like that."

"No problem, Baba. Happy to help. I'm just glad it got done."

"Me, too, but it might not have without you." I paused, considered leaving it at that. But my curiosity wouldn't let me. "How did you do it?" I asked, almost like an eager student. "What did you say to them?"

Humayun shrugged. "Not much, really," he said. "It's just that, sometimes, we all need a little direction."

The lady who cleaned the barracks at Fort Knox burst into a playful laugh when Ghazala introduced herself.

"Oh, Lieutenant Khan's mother!" she said. "I love to clean his room, because there's never anything for me to do! That's when I get to rest."

Then she spread her arms wide, stepped forward, and swung them around Ghazala, wrapping her in a tight hug. "You did such a wonderful job," she said. "He's such a fine young man."

It was Christmastime 2000, and Ghazala and Omer had gone to visit Humayun in Kentucky, where he'd been sent for his advanced officer training. Work kept me from going with them, but she told me that story when she returned, beaming with pride. What mother wouldn't? We hadn't seen him since May, when he got his degree from UVA and his second lieutenant's bars from the Army. There was a ceremony in the Rotunda, eight Army ROTC cadets turned out in their dress uniforms, brass buttons gleaming against olive suits, shoes spit-shiny black, the brims of their service caps anchored with a strip of gold braid. Maybe because the class was so small, maybe because of the solemnity of the oath they each were about to swear, the morning seemed intimate, as if we were all catching a glimpse of a secret ritual.

Humayun was the executive officer for his cadre, the number two person, the one who needs to be organized and level-headed. But even then, he seemed destined to lead more with his heart than with his head. He wrote a few words for the occasion:

During a recent Dining In, a wise man said, "The Army is about People." Leadership must be about dealing with people. An NCO told me, "If you have half a soldier's heart, you must love your soldiers. Take care of them, they will take care of you." They don't seem to care how much you know, until they know how much you care. What I found most valuable in ROTC is people. I enjoyed working with our cadets. My source of happiness is friendship. I've found success not a harbor, but a voyage, with its own perils of the spirit. The game of life is to achieve that which you set out to do. There is always danger of failing. The lesson that most of us on this voyage never learn, but can never quite forget, is that to win is sometimes to lose. Don't lose sight of your humanness. The Army is about people.

Humayun's brothers pinned his bars to the shoulders of his uniform, Omer and Shaharyar flanking him, each with a single gold-plated bar to affix. Once all of the cadets had been commissioned, they filed outside, under the portico at the top of the

Rotunda steps. A sergeant was waiting for them, one of the NCOs who had helped get the cadets through ROTC. Until a moment earlier, he'd outranked all of them. Now he was a subordinate, standing at attention to give each fresh lieutenant his first salute. One by one, the newly minted officers approached, snapped a crisp salute in return, then gave the sergeant a silver dollar, a traditional token of respect and gratitude.

As I watched from the bottom of the steps, it occurred to me that that sergeant might have the most bittersweet job in all of the military. He was not unlike a parent, I thought, hoping that his lessons had been absorbed, that his cadets were now capable officers. From the sharpness of his salute, it was obvious he believed in each of them, and that we should, too.

After graduation, Humayun was posted to Fort Lewis, near Tacoma, Washington, for a few weeks to work with ROTC cadets, and then sent to Fort Knox. There were a number of parties when Ghazala and Omer visited, it being the holidays, including one at the home of Humayun's commanding officer, a colonel. He invited Humayun, told him to bring his mother and brother. Any ambitious young second lieutenant who wanted to ingratiate himself with his superiors would have been there.

"We're not going to go, Mom," he said.

"What?" Ghazala recognized the invitation as the honor it was. "He's your commander. Why wouldn't you go?"

"Because my sergeant is having a party, too," he said. "No one's going to miss me at the colonel's. There'll be plenty of people there. But my sergeant, he would miss me. He'll be happy to see us, and that's where I belong."

Ghazala couldn't argue with that. Was it the savvy career move? Probably not. But was it the right thing to do, staying close to his men, even in something unofficial, a casual social gathering? Wasn't it just as he'd said when he was commissioned? *They don't care how much you know until they know how much you care.*

Yes, of course it was. Humayun sent his regrets to the colonel and took his mother and brother to his sergeant's home that night. The sergeant's face lit up when he opened the door. And his wife was so delighted, so touched that the lieutenant had brought his family, that she kissed Ghazala and nearly smothered her in a hug.

Maybe Ghazala was exaggerating. Maybe the sergeant was just pleasantly surprised. It was a small moment in one passing evening.

But what mattered is what Ghazala saw, which was that her boy had grown into a fine American lieutenant. He knew where he could have gone, and he knew where he belonged, and he never hesitated to go there instead. That's just how he was.

Humayun owed the Army four years, most of which he spent in Vilseck, Germany, assigned to the 201st Forward Support Battalion of the 1st Infantry Division. I don't know a lot about what he did there day in and day out, but he wasn't in a combat zone, which was a tremendous relief. While he was there, the United States invaded Afghanistan after the September 11, 2001, attacks on the World Trade Center and the Pentagon, and then Iraq in March 2003. But Humayun's unit was deployed only to Kosovo, to help maintain security for a few months starting in late 2002. For all practical purposes, he was serving peacetime duty, part of the massive American defense establishment spread around the globe, always prepared for war even if most of the military isn't required to go fight.

He was still a soldiers' officer. He'd been offered a position as a general's executive officer, an aide-de-camp, basically, a prestigious position that would have benefited his career, giving him a firmer grasp on the military chain of command and making it easier to climb. But he declined, just as he'd sent his regrets to a colonel's party to be with a sergeant. He was loyal to the men and women serving under him, felt responsible for them. To be an executive officer might have been good for him, but what would it do for his soldiers? What would it say to his soldiers? That his own advancement, a title and the reflected glow of a general's stars, was more important than they were? Maybe no one would have objected or felt slighted. But he'd written something important when he was commissioned: *Take care of your soldiers, and they will take care of you.* And so he did.

The most important thing he did in Germany was fall in love. Her name was Irene, and he met her in 2002 in a café in a little town called Amberg, not far from Vilseck. She said later that she was at first impressed with the way he spoke, in proper English, like a gentleman, not in the gibbering slang of so many Americans. They started dating, and within a few months she was spending the weekends with Humayun.

Ghazala met her in the spring of 2003, when she and Omer flew to Germany to visit. Irene's parents invited them all to their home for dinner, which was a fair indication of how serious Humayun was about her. I realize the culture of Pakistan in the early 1970s does not transpose cleanly to Europe thirty years later, but it's a universal truth that young men do not introduce their mothers to the parents of women they are only casually dating. Ghazala was quite taken with Irene, and with her family, who she believed would be a fine addition to our own. "She is exactly the kind of daughter-in-law I would like to have," she told me.

Not that we were pushing Humayun to get married. Quite the opposite. Just as my grandfather had impressed the importance of education on me, we pushed our boys to complete theirs. Indeed, we did our best to avoid anything that would distract from their studies. Neither Humayun nor Shaharyar, for instance, had a driver's license until after graduating from UVA. They didn't need the burden of driving friends around or looking after a car; if they wanted to come home for the weekend, we saw it as our responsibility to drive to Charlottesville, pick them up, and then ferry them back. Humayun was an adult, of course, and I couldn't control his life. But I hoped he would finish his tour in the Army, get his law degree, and then think about marriage and children. After all, no one knew better than me the difficulty of juggling a family and an education.

But I, too, was taken with Irene, whom I met a few months later, in September, when Humayun brought her to Virginia on leave. Ghazala cooked Humayun's favorite foods the night they arrived, ground beef mixed with split chickpeas and spices, with a side of boiled rice. Over dinner I met Irene, a lovely green-eyed blonde who spoke perfect English with a German accent that reminded me of Lisa's, Allen's wife in Dubai.

We stayed up visiting, just the sort of small talk people share when they're getting to know one another. She was a student, studying business, and she clearly adored Humayun. She told us how he was not only a commander but also a counselor, the captain whom soldiers came to with their troubles. She recognized, and seemed to cherish, the softer side of him, the part of Humayun that wanted to understand people, what motivated and comforted them. That was, in fact, what Humayun enjoyed most about the Army, working with people. He told me he wanted to make the military a career, that after he finished law school he would reenlist, become a military lawyer.

Early the next morning, when I was getting ready for work, Humayun and Irene were lacing up their running shoes. They stretched on the front steps, then trotted off into the neighborhood. I finished getting ready, got in my car, and started the drive into D.C. I could see Humayun coming toward me, jogging at a pretty good clip, but alone. I stopped, rolled down the window.

"Where is Irene?"

He laughed. "She runs so slow," he said. He looked over his shoulder. "There she is," he said. "She's coming. But slowly." He laughed again.

I decided to drive off, so as not to embarrass her, this lovely young lady I'd only just met. That evening, though, I asked her if she was okay after her morning run.

She laughed, too. "Oh, yes, I'm fine," she said. "He just runs so fast to show off when I'm with him."

That was probably true. But she took it in good humor, as if she was on to him, knew he was strutting, trying to impress her. She had an easy nature, an openness that seemed neither self-conscious nor practiced. If Ghazala — whom she respectfully but never obsequiously always called Mrs. Khan — was in the kitchen preparing a meal or cleaning up, Irene would join her. A woman trying too hard would say, "Let me do this." Irene just fell into a rhythm alongside her, doing what needed to be done but never insisting on taking over. It was a small thing, but the sort of gesture parents notice. After only a short visit, I agreed with Ghazala: Irene would be a wonderful daughter-in-law, though I hoped they would wait until after Humayun passed the bar.

"You know I am against this war," I told Humayun.

He creased his mouth into a tight smile, nodded. "I know," he said. "But I can't think like that."

He was in Bristow again, on his last leave from the Army before being scheduled to muster out in June 2004, only six months away. Then he would start applying to law schools. That's what he'd said, that's what the deal had been, when he was a college freshman, sitting in the springtime sun with his parents, telling his mother not to worry, that there were no wars being fought, that he could die just as easily riding a motorcycle on Interstate 66, that it was all a matter of destiny and fate. And destiny had been kind. When the awful crimes of September 11 happened and the United States overthrew the Taliban in Afghanistan, Humayun was safe in Europe. When the U.S. government argued, persuasively if incorrectly, that Saddam Hussein was hiding weapons of mass destruction and then invaded Iraq purportedly to find them, Humayun was a captain in charge of a tank platoon, but his unit was not deployed to the Middle East. He'd remained, through two invasions, in Germany.

But the winds of fate had shifted. A month earlier, in November 2003, the soldiers in Humayun's division had been notified that they would be rotated into Iraq.

"We shouldn't even be fighting in Iraq," I said. "We have nothing to gain as a country."

Humayun didn't say anything right away. He just looked at me. What could he say? That I was right? Wrong? I don't know which he thought, and neither would have mattered. He was a soldier, not a pundit.

War is always a tragedy, visceral and bloody evidence that all other options have failed. And yet it is often discomfitingly popular: When the air strikes began on Baghdad in March 2003, almost 70 percent of Americans approved. The war was televised, like a miniseries, and grainy videos from the noses of precision-guided missiles aired in loops, like highlight reels. Magnets twisted into yellow ribbons were ubiquitous

291

on SUVS and sedans. France opposed the invasion, so a congressman (a corrupt one, it turned out) ordered three Capitol Hill cafeterias to start serving Freedom Fries instead of french fries. The line separating patriotism from jingoism became badly blurred.

But war is also much easier to cheer from a safe remove. There had been a slight increase in military enlistments after 9/11 — though nothing like after, say, the bombing of Pearl Harbor — but by the end of 2003, the military was stretched so thin that stop-loss orders were being issued. That means what it sounds like: In order to stop losing fighters, the military would force service members to stay beyond their scheduled enlistment. On November 13, the Army put a stop-loss on about 110,000 soldiers, including my son. His tour in Iraq would last until the Army decided to end it.

"This isn't right," I persisted. "This war, it is wrong. It does not serve the interests of my country. Quite the contrary, it causes harm to our national interest."

That was not a new belief on my part; I did not decide invading Iraq was a bad idea only because my son was being sent there. Nor am I necessarily a pacifist. I am, however, a student of history and of Islam.

When the Prophet, peace be upon him, died in the early seventh century, there was a dispute over who should succeed him. A minority of Muslims, the Shi'a, believed the Prophet had chosen his cousin and son-in-law Ali as his heir; Sunnis, meanwhile, maintained that Abu Bakr, a companion of the Prophet, was his rightful successor. The repercussions of that split — theological, cultural, social — have been reverberating for fourteen hundred years. Iraq is one of the few places where Shi'a predominate, yet for years they were ruled by a Sunni despot. I knew, as anyone with a basic understanding of Islam knew, that removing Saddam Hussein, no matter how righteous that cause might be in theory, risked unleashing centuries of resentments and bitterness into an ugly civil war.

I was at a loss to explain what interest my country had in such an event.

"I know, Baba," Humayun said finally. "But I can't think in those terms. I'm an officer in the Army. My responsibility is to the men and women under my command."

I understood. I certainly wasn't telling him not to go. I wasn't even trying to persuade him to my point of view. But he was my son, and I was afraid. I couldn't say that out loud, couldn't show it, so I diverted those emotions into something larger, more abstract. Maybe I hoped that would make the danger smaller, less concrete. I had to be strong — for Humayun, for his brothers, for Ghazala — just as Humayun had to be strong for us.

He knew Ghazala was sick with worry. "Don't be a hero," she told him. "Please, don't be a hero."

He took her hands in his. "Mom, my job is to keep people safe," he said. That was true: His unit was going to be in charge of securing a sprawling base near Baqubah, in the Diyala province north of Baghdad. "And I can't keep people safe if I'm not safe, right? So when you think of it that way, I have to be the safest person there."

Ghazala tried to smile, but she seemed unconvinced — not of his skills or his caution, but of the whims of fate. No one is ever really in control of a war.

He stayed with us for a couple of weeks. We tried not to talk much about where he was going. There was no point in burdening our days together with constant worries about what we could not control. We are people of strong faith. We could only bow our heads and hope for divine guidance and protection.

The four of us — Ghazala, myself, his

brothers — took Humayun to the airport for his flight back to Germany. He didn't look like a soldier, dressed in jeans and a sweater, but anyone watching him walk, who saw the way he stood at the United Airlines counter, confident, with perfect posture, could probably guess.

He was checking his duffel bag and a pair of boxes, so he put them on the scale beside the check-in agent. He'd filled the boxes with books to occupy his time in Iraq, so many that Ghazala warned him they might be too heavy. She was right. The agent told him he had to lighten one of the boxes, shift some books to his bag. Humayun squatted down and pulled open the box. He turned his head toward Ghazala and gave her that half smirk and the slow nod, his way of saying the joke was on him, that he should have listened to his mother.

Ghazala was trying not to cry.

I've always thought that, through her faith, she was closer to our Creator. And I've always thought such people sometimes have inclinations, not premonitions so much as hunches.

I tried to forget that I thought that.

We walked him as far as the security checkpoint, beyond which we couldn't follow. I told him to stay safe, stay strong. He hugged his mother last, and for a moment I thought she might not let go. Shaharyar put a hand on her shoulder and gently pulled her away. Tears welled in her eyes as she watched Humayun walk into the queue. I reached for her, turned her, started walking away. "You can't let him see you," I whispered. "We need to strengthen him, not burden him."

We kept walking. That is what military families do when they send a child off to war. They put on a brave face for as long as they can, and then they look the other way.

Humayun called from Iraq on Mother's Day. He was a captain in the United States Army in the middle of a war zone, but he was still his mother's son.

He had deployed to Diyala in February, and we'd been able to speak only a few times since and never for very long. There were always soldiers waiting for the phone to call their worried parents and spouses, girlfriends and boyfriends. He could have pulled rank, stayed on the line as long as he wanted, but a captain's duty is also to maintain the morale of the men and women he commanded, so his Mother's Day call wasn't very long. Ghazala, relieved and delighted to hear his voice, safe and calm, reminded him not to be a hero.

I asked him if he'd received the book I'd sent in April, Senator John McCain's *Why Courage Matters: The Way to a Braver Life*. McCain had always been one of Humayun's heroes, a fighter pilot and prisoner of war who suffered for almost six years in Hanoi. The North Vietnamese offered to release him because McCain's father was an admiral, but he refused: POWs were supposed to be sent home in the order they were captured, not according to the privilege of their birth. He stayed in prison because it was the honorable thing, the *right* thing, to do.

Why Courage Matters was the senator's third book, and it is primarily profiles of people he believes have shown extraordinary courage. His point, the theme running throughout, is that "courage" had become an overused term, tossed off too easily, accepted too readily. Simply overcoming fear can be brave, but it can also be a cheap stunt, like walking on hot coals or bungee-jumping from a bridge. True courage, by contrast, requires sacrifice and, quite often, physical risk for the benefit of others.

"Yeah, I got it, Baba," he said. "Thank you. I'm about halfway through it."

"Okay, good," I said. I tried to keep my voice steady. "Stay strong. Stay safe."

He said that he would.

My mother lived with us in Bristow, as she had for years, ever since we'd been in Maryland. My blessed father had died of heart disease in 1979, and my siblings had pitched in to run the farm and take care of my mother. But once I became a citizen, I was able to sponsor her for a resident visa. She moved to the United States in the early 1990s, and once she was settled and enough time had passed, she was allowed to sponsor my siblings, all nine of them. I remember filling out all the applications, probably around 1993, and driving her to the immigration office, where we took a number, found two seats, and waited to be called.

An immigration officer, a heavyset black woman with a kind face, summoned my mother. I got up with her.

"You can't come," the officer said.

"Please," I said. "She doesn't speak English very well, and she might need me to translate."

The officer eyed me for a moment, winked, and jerked her head for me to follow. "Okay, c'mon," she said.

She slid behind her desk, opened my mother's file, and paged through the applications. She looked up, looked back at the file, flipped through the pages again. She got up and came around to our side of the desk with the biggest, warmest smile I'd ever seen in a government office. She bent down and wrapped her arms around my mother.

"I just had to hug you," she said. "You raised nine" — she looked quickly at me — "you raised ten children. That is so, so wonderful. You're a saint."

My mother *was* a saint. I was overjoyed when she moved in with us. One reason, of course, was that she was my mother and I loved her. Yet she was also my children's grandmother, and I wanted our boys to grow up in her company, wanted them to be grounded in their own family history. Memories are preserved in the generations that come before us, and without those memories, it is easy for one to become lost, to lose perspective on their place in the endless cycle of creation. I wanted our children to understand who we were as they became who they would be.

And there was another reason: My mother was Ghazala's closest friend. I think she always had been, since that first walk in Lahore so many years ago. Both of my parents had embraced Ghazala as their own daughter. My father, who used to hide his smoking from his own mother, used to offer her a cigarette, a courtesy he never extended to me. Years later, in Maryland and then Virginia, Ghazala and my mother would stay up late, after everyone else had gone to bed, and then drive off to Dunkin' Donuts to sit in the neon light sipping coffee and eating doughnuts. It was almost a ritual, time away from everyone else, just the two of them, talking about things they never told me. It was sweet, my mother and my wife being so close.

On one bright green afternoon in June, my mother caught a glimpse of movement outside our house. From the window, she saw two men in military uniform coming up the front walk.

She called for Ghazala, fear in her voice.

Ghazala came to the window.

She knew why officers came in pairs.

She collapsed to the floor.

"Mr. Khan?"

I didn't recognize the voice on the other end of the phone, but that wasn't unusual. I was at the office and got calls from all sorts of people. "Yes, this is him."

The voice told me he was an Army chaplain. He apologized for calling me at work.

My stomach knotted. My pulse quickened.

The oxygen in the room suddenly seemed very thin.

"I have some very tragic news," he said.

I'm sure there was a pause. Seconds? Minutes? How does one measure time when it stops?

"I've been notified that Captain Khan has been killed. How soon can you come home?"

"How is Mrs. Khan?" She was my first thought.

"She's fainted, but she's okay."

"Please, don't leave her," I said. "My mother is with her, but she doesn't speak English well. Please wait until I get there."

Every motion was instinct after that. I called a family friend, asked her to get to the house as quickly as possible. I got to my car, started it, drove from muscle memory. I remember being calm, but I was numb. *This didn't happen,* I told myself. *This could not have happened to Humayun. This could not happen to Captain Humayun Khan.*

This is not real.

I repeated those thoughts in my head, or maybe out loud, all the way home. I was certain my son was not dead. The military is a bureaucracy, I knew, a giant organization spread all over the planet. Papers get misfiled in every bureaucracy. Mistakes hap-

301

pen. This was a mistake.

This could not happen to Captain Humayun Khan.

There was no need to be angry, I thought. I would not be upset when this situation, this grievous misunderstanding, was straightened out. I would tell the officers I forgave them, that I understood it was a terrible mix-up. *No, there is no need to apologize,* I would say. These things happen. I would tell them that I would pray for the family of the soldier who had died, the soldier who was not Captain Humayun Khan.

Shaharyar and Omer were at the house, stricken, almost in shock. Ghazala was inconsolable. Friends filtered in. Television trucks crept down the street; reporters gathered on the lawn.

The war had been going on for more than a year, but a soldier from a small town killed in combat was still news then, and being close to a major media market made it easy for reporters to find us. But so quickly? They all wanted us to say something, and they were polite and respectful, insofar as one can be polite and respectful while intruding on a stranger's immediate, overwhelming grief. And what did anyone expect us to say? That he was a wonderful son, that we were completely shattered, that the pain was so intense that it paralyzed rational thought, blurred the world into a slow, thick slurry?

We sent a friend out to read a short statement asking for privacy.

I did not grieve for Humayun, because I did not believe he was dead. The Army chaplain told us he had been killed in an explosion, but I knew they were wrong. And what if they weren't? What if I was wrong, what if Humayun really had been killed?

I could not grieve then, either, not yet. A darkness had swallowed our lives, had swarmed over us, extraordinarily fast and pitiless. My wife and my sons were suddenly, utterly lost, disoriented, groping in the dark. Who would stand strong? Who would guide them, comfort them? When everyone is falling apart, someone has to keep himself together.

What would Captain Humayun Khan do?

You assume the role, no matter how broken you are inside.

My son was in a coffin.

I saw him, looked at him, stared at him. He was my son. My beautiful boy.

For days, I'd continued to convince myself the Army was wrong. Even on the drive to the funeral home, I told myself there had been a terrible mistake. An Army casualty officer, a captain, drove me, and only me; I was still the stoic one in the family because I had to be. I knew that when we got there, when we saw the body in the casket, I would shake with relief and gratitude. Then I would tell them to go, hurry, go to the family that needs you, the family of this poor, lost soldier.

The captain stood behind me as I approached the casket. He stood at attention, saluting.

A sudden tranquillity interrupted my thinking. I nodded slightly. "Yes," I said. "That's my son." Because it was.

It is a cliché, but he looked peaceful, as if he was sleeping, perhaps even dreaming of something pleasant. There were no marks or blemishes on his smooth brown skin. The dimple in his chin was unmarred. The only unusual detail was the bandage, a bright white stripe of gauze stretched across his forehead, covering the wound where a piece of shrapnel had hit him above his left eye.

Humayun had been deployed to a forward operating base called Camp Warhorse. Tuesday, June 8, was his day off, but he went out to the main gate that morning to check on his soldiers, who were responsible for, among other things, security. It was early, about eight o'clock, what everyone called rush hour because of the Iraqi civilians arriving for work. The camp employed about a thousand locals, which was both practical — work needed to be done — and strategic: Giving people jobs improved the local economy, which in turn improved living conditions, and people in general are less likely to see as enemies the soldiers who are giving them, or their fathers or mothers or brothers, a paycheck.

The Americans were never meant to be the Iraqis' enemy. That would become easy to forget as the war dragged on, but the point of invading Iraq was supposed to have been liberating the population from a despot, not subjugating it to American imperialism. It was right there in the name: Operation Iraqi Freedom.

Still, by the late spring of 2004, an insurgency had taken root, and Diyala province was one of the seeding grounds. Camp Warhorse had been repeatedly attacked. Security was abundant and tight. There were a series of barriers and gates, a course of deliberate obstructions, leading from the main road. Vehicles were stopped and inspected, mirrors sweeping the undercarriage, the engine compartment and trunk poked through. Civilians parked in a fenced lot set well back from the perimeter of the camp proper. Vehicles coming into the base had to pass though a long canyon of blast walls laid out with sharp turns that forced drivers to maneuver through them at a crawl. Towers flanked the path, .50-caliber machine guns tracking anything moving.

Sometimes, rarely, a car slipped through, the driver refusing to stop, ignoring the warnings.

On that Tuesday morning, it was an orange taxi with a driver and a passenger. One of the guards notified Captain Khan.

Humayun could have told his soldiers in the towers to put a few rounds through the windshield and into the engine block. He could have ordered the taxi destroyed, the driver and his passenger killed. If the vehicle was a threat, a short burst of gunfire could easily have stopped it.

But what if the taxi wasn't a threat? What if the driver was confused, didn't understand what all those foreigners were yelling, didn't know if all the arm-waving meant stop or go, come on or turn around? What if he was just trying to get some poor guy to work so he could earn a few bucks for his family?

Humayun still could have told his soldiers

to shoot him. That would have been perfectly legal. It also would have been prudent. It was hardly his fault that some Iraqi driver got confused. It had happened before, happened right in that very canyon of blast walls, happened a hundred times, a thousand times, all over Iraq. People die in wars. Mistakes, awful and tragic mistakes, are made.

Captain Khan told everyone to stay back. He started walking toward the taxi, his arms up, a universal sign to stop. He wasn't going to kill a man by mistake. He believed in his mission, the overarching point of which was to bring freedom and safety to people in a country where they'd had neither. He would tell Iraqis that, directly and explicitly. "We're not here to hurt you," he would say. "We are here to help you." He and other officers had organized local men to patrol Baqubah, the provincial capital, paid them five dollars an hour to go out with American soldiers, to make them part of their own security, their own destiny.

How much damage would two dead civilians cause? How much of that work would be destroyed?

He took a few more steps, arms still up. I was told he took ten steps, but I don't know if anyone actually counted.

He saw something. Maybe a look on the driver's face, maybe the explosives packed around him.

Captain Khan turned, yelled for everyone to hit the dirt.

The taxi exploded. The concussion killed him instantly, almost certainly before the shrapnel even hit him. Two Iraqi civilians close to the car were killed, too, and ten soldiers were wounded.

And now my son was in a coffin, a white bandage on his forehead, peaceful, at rest.

The Army said he was a hero, awarded him a Bronze Star and a Purple Heart. Who knows how many would have died if the taxi had gotten closer to the gate? How many other fathers' children weren't in coffins? Dozens? Does the number matter? Is one enough?

But there was also this: My son was dead because he was trying to make sure a stranger wasn't killed by mistake. He stayed true to the shape of his heart.

Humayun Saqib Muazzam Khan, a most fortunate one, destined for greatness, a king who would shine among the heavens. He was, and I believe he does.

I studied his face, so young, so kind. I did not think of those things in that moment. I'm not sure what I thought of, or if I thought at all. Pride can be a balm, but it is not immediately effective, and it never, ever heals the wound.

Our son's headstone is a slab of white marble with soft streaks the color of wood smoke, a rectangle except for the top, which is rounded off in a shallow arc. A star nestled inside a crescent moon is etched at the top, above his name, his rank and branch of service, the date of his birth and the date of his death, the medals the Army awarded him, and the conflict, Operation Iraqi Freedom, in which he died.

Twenty-seven years reduced to eleven carved lines.

It was placed in Section 60 of Arlington National Cemetery, at the end of a row of other marble headstones that condense the lives of other sons and daughters into too few chiseled words. Humayun was buried there one week after he was killed, on June 15, a hot, clear day on the eve of summer. The deputy chief of mission from the Pakistani embassy was there; Humayun was the highest-ranking Pakistani American to die in Iraq. An Army chaplain read a letter from Humayun's commanding officer, who was still overseas. "He died selflessly and courageously, tackling the enemy head on,"

Lieutenant Colonel Dan Mitchell had written. "We will not forget him and the noble ideas he stood for."

I believed that was true. I hoped that was true.

A bugler played Taps. Six officers in dress uniforms lifted the flag covering my son's casket and folded it into a tight triangle. One of them carried it, gently, as if it were a fragile thing that might shatter, to Ghazala, clicked his heels, bent forward, and held it out to her. She accepted it, tears streaming down her cheeks.

There would be other memorials. Two in Charlottesville over the summer, another at Fort Knox in the fall, where we would sit in a grandstand and look out over young lieutenants in formation on the parade ground. "They all look like Humayun," Ghazala would whisper to me, and she would be right. Their uniforms, their posture.

They each were someone's child.

Another soldier was buried in Arlington the same day as Humayun, a sergeant first class from Louisiana, Army Special Forces, who'd been killed in Afghanistan two weeks earlier. That was a private ceremony, but there were reporters at ours. We were able to talk by then. Ghazala told *The Washington*

Post how she had cried every time she spoke to Humayun. I explained how he died, as best I understood it. "Where did his strength come from to face such a danger instead of hiding behind a pole or a booth or something?" I said. "Normally, we would try to hide. Had he done that, there would be no problem at all. It may not have been fatal."

Irene was there. She'd flown from Germany. In one of Humayun's last emails to her, he'd asked her to look for an engagement ring. "He was perfect," Irene told the reporter. "He was the most wonderful person I've ever met."

There was a story on the front page of the metro section the next morning. A "PEACE-MAKER" IS LAID TO REST, the headline said. We were grateful for the tone, for an opportunity to say a few words, and that strangers knew, at least for one morning, a little bit of our son.

But what more was there to say? What more did anyone need to know, want to know?

Nothing. Our lives had been shattered, but the world hadn't changed. The war would continue. Thousands more would die. In the grand sweep of history, Captain Humayun Khan would be a footnote, a name on a creeping list of the dead, on a marble headstone planted in a wide and endless lawn. Our pain was immeasurable, but it was not the public's pain.

We went home to be alone with our grief, to begin to make peace with a specter we knew would never leave.

CHAPTER 10
ALWAYS BE A RIVER

A car pulled up the black top driveway, followed by two gray vans, the elongated ones with eighteen seats. The colonel in charge of the Army ROTC program at UVA got out of his sedan, waited while cadets in fatigues and tan boots filed out of the vans and formed themselves into a line. Then he led them up the stone steps of our new Charlottesville house, past the azaleas, thick and green with late summer leaves, a parade of young soldiers passing in front of our big bay window.

Fourteen months had passed since Captain Humayun Khan had been killed in Iraq. We didn't stay in Bristow long after that. The house was too familiar, too tainted with grief, and our other sons were in Charlottesville, where Shaharyar had started a business after graduating from medical school and where Omer was working with him. Ghazala wanted to be closer to the

313

children who remained, and the grand-children we expected would come someday. So did I.

We'd primarily looked at houses on the west side of the city, but our real estate agent showed us one on the east side, on the southern slope of Carter Mountain, which we chose. Monticello, Thomas Jefferson's home, isn't far, on top of the mountain, and local lore says he hid in the woods near our house when the British came looking for him after he signed the Declaration of Independence. The house is on a quiet street, but when the trees are bare or just starting to bud, we can see across the neighborhood to the traffic passing on State Route 20. More than two hundred years ago, Jefferson and James Madison, whose Montpelier is just north of Charlottesville, used to travel that same road to each other's homes when they were helping to birth a nation. There are green signs planted now every few miles that read CONSTITUTION ROUTE.

Fate is a curious thing. The young law student who'd first read Jefferson's words in a shaft of sunlight in Lahore was now a middle-aged lawyer living in the shadow of Jefferson's home. That wasn't planned; it was serendipity, nothing more.

■ ■ ■ ■

A few weeks earlier, the colonel had asked if he could bring all of his Army cadets to pay their respects to Humayun. It was important, he felt, to remind students who would swear an oath to defend the Constitution, who would be deployed as officers in the military, that such a commitment came with risk. That was not to frighten anyone, of course, but to remind them that sacrifice is sometimes required and must always be honored.

No one would have begrudged us if we'd retreated, if we'd put as much distance between ourselves and the military as possible, not out of bitterness but as a matter of emotional self-preservation. But we didn't see it that way.

The truth is that we considered those cadets and their instructors to be part of our extended family, young people who held the same ideals, aspired to the same goals, as Humayun. We felt, in a way, a responsibility to them. We'd already established, the previous spring, the Captain Humayun Khan Leadership Award to be presented to the outstanding graduating cadet from UVA's Army ROTC class. It came with a

$1,000 stipend — we'd considered perhaps a plaque or some other memento, but we were told that what a newly commissioned second lieutenant needed most was cash — and we'd funded it in perpetuity. And we'd given each of that year's graduates a gift — a copy of *Why Courage Matters* that I ordered from a local bookstore and that Senator McCain had graciously signed. Ghazala wrapped each one, tying flowers to the paper, double-checking the spelling of each cadet's name.

So what if you are thirsty? Always be a river for everyone.

Humayun's death was, and still is, and always will be, devastating. I realize I am expected to put our grief into words, to find a metaphor that will give shape and form and color to what is an immutable and eternal void. I cannot. I do not know the words to describe such agony, and I do not wish to learn them.

But we are people of faith. We bow our heads and try to see the divine plan. I remembered my grandfather's lessons, that God is to be found in people and that the Creator has appointed everyone a station in life. Humayun had found his station. The Creator had allowed us to be custodians of him for twenty-seven years, and now, surely, his soul lived on. Perhaps his station had become a source of strength and inspiration to young officers. We can only be grateful for the twenty-seven years we had with him, and pray that he is with us still, even if it is in ways we cannot fully understand.

The colonel and the cadets came in the front door, greeted us as *ma'am* and *sir,* though with a humility and warmth not usually associated with such formalities. They turned left into the sitting room bright with August light flooding through the bay window.

This was the room we had dedicated to Humayun. On the wall opposite the windows, Omer and I had hung his diplomas from UVA and the Army's armor school and, in the center, a photograph of a tank matted into a frame above a lieutenant's bar and a brass nameplate that read LT. HUMAYUN S. KHAN, "BLUE 6," BANDIT THIRD PLATOON LEADER. In the center of the far wall was a portrait of him in his dress uniform. We'd hung other significant documents and insignia next to it and in a row below, Omer and I carefully measuring where we tapped in the hooks, keeping everything level and evenly spaced, orderly, tidy, just as Humayun would have. Our Gold Star flag — a field of white bordered by red with a single star in the center — was to the right of his portrait. Beneath his portrait was another Gold Star flag, this one with gold fringe at the bottom, and a picture of him the day he was commissioned above the words he'd written for the occasion. The *Washington Post* story from the day after his burial was next to that. On a table below, there was a photo of Humayun and his brothers, taken moments after they'd pinned the bars on his uniform.

The wall is exactly the same as I write this. I study it occasionally, stare at my boy's face, his ribbons, his tributes. I catch myself now and again, realize that I half expect something might have changed, that a frame might have moved, exposed a fresh spot on the wall. But nothing ever changes.

Ghazala remained in the foyer. She wouldn't go into that room then. She knew emotion would overwhelm her, swallow her. Omer would usually tend to it, vacuuming and dusting and straightening.

"Welcome," I said to the cadets once they'd all filed in. "In each and every one of you, we see a reflection of Humayun." I blinked hard, swallowed. All those young faces, so honorable. So much promise. "You remind us of him so much that it's as if he's in the other room, and he'll appear at any moment with his smile."

I blinked again. He would not appear. They knew he would not appear.

The cadets studied the photos and the tributes, standing at ease, hands clasped behind their backs as they moved around the room, as if they were examining masterpieces in a hallowed museum. No one spoke. It was somber but not gloomy. Respectful, honorable.

We didn't want the cadets to leave without a gift. We'd already started a tradition of giving the McCain books to graduates, so more books wouldn't do. I'd pondered what to present them for weeks, flummoxed, trying to think of something meaningful but not ponderous or ostentatious. That puzzle still sat unsolved in the back of my mind one afternoon when I was flipping through the *ABA Journal,* the magazine of the American Bar Association. An ad caught my eye: pocket Constitutions, ninety-nine cents each if you bought ten or more.

I ordered fifty.

I held a stack as I stood near the front door. "Each of you will be taking an oath soon to defend this Constitution," I said, holding one up. "Please read it as you prepare to defend it" — my voice hitched — "as you prepare to defend it, regardless of the cost."

The azaleas and the redbuds bloomed again, spring flowering the slopes of Carter Mountain. Ghazala wrapped books for another class of graduating Army cadets, fine young second lieutenants who received their first salute from a sergeant on the portico of the Rotunda. Then summer came, sticky and hot, and with it another platoon of cadets filing past the bushes and through the foyer and into the room with Humayun's pictures and our Gold Star flags.

We fed them that year, 2006, a proper meal instead of the cookies and soft drinks we'd offered the first time. This contribution, cooking for young people, was Ghazala's idea, as if she was feeding Humayun's friends again the way she did when he was a boy, laying out hamburgers and french fries. She still rarely went into the room with the bay windows, and if she did — to straighten or to dust — she did so quickly, looking anywhere but at Humayun's portrait, his soft brown eyes staring down from the wall. To engage them, to let her gaze linger, would be devastating to her, a reminder of what we had lost. But the cadets paying their respects brought her some comfort.

"It's as if Humayun has lit a candle," she told me once, "and all of these young people are coming to light their own candles from his."

For years the cadets came to our home every summer and we went to their graduation every spring. Those occasions were solemn, but not depressing, as they were less a reminder of what we'd lost than of what Humayun had achieved, of what he aspired to and represented, of the twenty-seven years we'd been blessed with him. In any case, it was impossible to remind us of our loss because it was ever present, a shadow that would darken to a deep black some days and might lighten ever so slightly on others but would never fade completely away.

We got on with our lives as best we could, smoothing the hard edges of our grief until it became a chronic ache rather than an acute, debilitating pain. That was a private process, kept within the family and shared only with a few close friends. Even among the cadets, making their respectful pilgrimages each August, we did not speak of our sadness. They were training to be officers, not casualties; they had come to honor Hu-

mayun's service, not to pity our devasta-
tion.

CHAPTER 11
GOD IS FOUND
AMONG THE PEOPLE

There used to be a fabric store in downtown Charlottesville called Les Fabriques, a short drive from our home off the Constitution Route. In the summer of 2005, Ghazala was sewing some clothing — she was still a gifted seamstress — and needed some new material, so she drove herself to the small mall on Water Street.

As she was paying, she started to cry. By way of explanation, she told the store's owner about Humayun, about what a wonderful son he'd been, how he'd grown into a fine young man and became an Army officer who served with honor and distinction, how he'd been sent to war and was killed while saving other people. "I've cried for a whole year," she said. "I have to get off my couch and stop crying."

The owner cried with her, the two of them weeping at the counter.

Grief often is described as an emptiness, a

void that can't be spackled over. But it's worse than that. It's a physical presence, a dark weight that settles over everything, a smothering shadow constantly reminding you of what has been lost. It is always there, impossible to remove, but we've found that it can be pushed aside. For a few hours at first, and in time those hours become days and then weeks. Grief never leaves, but its heaviness can be displaced. You get used to it, even if you never get comfortable with it.

In the months and years after Humayun was killed, I had my work to distract me, long hours burying myself in complex litigation; in time, an important client asked me to work full-time for them, and, since the money was better and I could set my own hours, I left the firm and became a consultant. Shaharyar and Omer had their work, too. We kept busy, and being busy gave us a counterbalance to our pain.

But Ghazala was alone in our home, her only companion during the day an enveloping darkness. She had no profession to occupy her mind, no office she could retreat to for a few hours.

Ghazala was, by training and nature, a scholar, and she would have been an exceptional professor. Had she chosen to teach, she would have been nearing retirement from a brilliant career when Humayun was sent to Iraq. But that was not what she'd wanted.

She had not worked since we left Pakistan. We'd discussed the prospect decades before, and many times in the years that followed. In some ways, I would have preferred it if Ghazala had taken a job. In Texas, when Shaharyar and Humayun were five and six and seemed to need new shoes and new clothes every few months, the extra income would have taken the financial burden off me. Money was always tight.

Yet the way Ghazala saw it — and I could not disagree — any money she earned would have come at a cost. When we were in Texas, a woman named Mrs. Singh operated a daycare center in our subdivision. We thought it might help acclimate our older boys to their new home to spend afternoons there. Since we were on a budget, Ghazala volunteered as a teacher in exchange for a fifty percent discount. She was assigned to a different room than Shaharyar and Humayun — Mrs. Singh had a policy about separating parents and their children — but she could hear Shaharyar wailing for her. (Humayun, sweetly enough, did not cry because, as he told Mrs. Singh, "My brother is crying for me, too.") In her own room,

Ghazala saw other children crying for their parents.

Most kids get over the temporary separation quickly enough. For some parents, two incomes are a necessity; for some, it is a beneficial trade-off, daycare and work. But it was not for Ghazala. "These children have been entrusted to us," she told me. "We brought them into the world, and we have only a short while with them. They are my most important job."

She saw the generations in the same way my grandmother did, each raised as the one before it had been, which meant she was reaching through our children far into the future, to her grandchildren and great-grandchildren and so on, into a future for which we could only hope to set a proper foundation.

So we lived with a little less. We did not have two cars and we did not have extensive wardrobes and we did without some small and, in the end, unnecessary luxuries. Ghazala drove the boys to school each morning and picked them up each afternoon and cooked for their friends and went to all the parent-teacher conferences and swim meets. When Shaharyar was chosen to be on his high school's *That's Academic* team — a quiz show for students — she was in the audience with Humayun and Omer every Saturday morning for three years. She was the anchor of our family. That our boys grew up to be such fine young men is because of her. My task was to make enough money to support us, and in many ways it was much easier than hers.

She might have grown restless once the boys had graduated college and started their own lives. Maybe she would have started working, or maybe she would have simply busied herself around the house or in the community, until the next generation arrived for her to dote on with the same endless affection. But with Humayun's death came that unbearable weight. And she sat with it, alone in the house, until she walked into Les Fabriques.

She began spending part of her week there, volunteering, answering questions about techniques and materials. Eventually, she went to work part-time, teaching sewing lessons. It was a salve, a few hours immersing herself in an art that she loved. She also continued sewing at home. She bought yards of billowy cream fabric that she stitched into curtains and adorned with tassels and trimmed with delicate ribbons, and we hung them around the big bay windows in the room with Humayun's honors and mementos. They filter the afternoon light, temper it, the way stained-glass panels soften the interior of a chapel.

After the cadets came to pay their respects the first time, I started keeping one of those Constitutions in the pocket of my suit coat. It wasn't for superstitious reasons, as if it were a talisman or a lucky charm, nor was it even a deliberate habit. In fact, I don't remember the first time I tucked it into my pocket, exactly when or the reason why.

It became a reflexive resource for me, part reference guide, part notebook. In time, I added two quotations to the inside of the back cover. The first, not surprisingly, is from Thomas Jefferson. "TJ," I wrote, in black pen, "1st sec of state, a lawyer, believed, 'Building a just and solid govt. at home would be the way the US would serve as an example to the world.' " Sometime later, I came across a line from Justice Antonin Scalia, whom I've always admired as a scholar even if I haven't always agreed with his opinions. "Rudimentary justice," he wrote in 1989, "requires that those subject to the law must have the means of knowing what it proscribes." That, it seemed to me, was a brilliantly concise argument for keeping the law as clear and simple as possible.

If I was with other lawyers and we were discussing a particular case, I would flip through and find where the applicable law was rooted. In 2005, for instance, a landmark case — *Kelo v. the City of New London* — went before the Supreme Court, concerning the government's ability to take a person's private property for the public good. Eminent domain, as it's known, has long been a contentious matter. Can the government really just take your land? Yes, within limits, says the last clause of the Fifth Amendment: "nor shall private property be taken for public use, without just compensation." I highlighted those twelve words in yellow and underlined *just compensation.* What does that mean, exactly? What is "just" when the government wants to demolish your home? There are libraries of case law on that question, and the answer is almost always specific to the circumstances. To me, though, it was an exercise in legal reasoning. And there was a magnificence in that: The law is ever evolving, and the seemingly plain meaning of the Constitution's words has been — and must be — repeatedly reinterpreted through the prism of the times. To understand the law — to have "the means of knowing what it proscribes," as Justice Scalia put it — almost requires such intellectual excercises.

The text of the Fourteenth Amendment begins on page 35 of my little Constitution. The page is creased, soft with age and handling, marked with fading yellow highlighter and notes scribbled in blue ballpoint ink. There is a thick pen stroke at the beginning of the second sentence of Section 1, followed by highlighting and underlining: "No State shall make or enforce any law which shall *abridge the privileges or immunities of citizens of the United States;* nor shall *any State deprive any person of life, liberty, or property, without due process of law; nor deny to any person within its jurisdiction the equal protection of the laws.*"

Those words are, to me, the essence of America, the culmination of everything those brave patriots set down in the Declaration of Independence, generations of struggle and sacrifice distilled to a single sentence. For the poor man, the immigrant, the homeless veteran living under a bridge, to be treated under the law the same as the rich man, the scion, the connected political appointee is the greatest privilege of being a United States citizen. It is what all people, everywhere, aspire to: the fundamental dignity of equality. When you live somewhere it doesn't exist, it is all you yearn for.

That is not an academic conclusion, a concept I memorized from books on the law or philosophy. Rather, I understand it honestly, organically. I am an American patriot not because I was born here but because I was not. I embraced American freedoms, raised my children to cherish and revere them, lost a son who swore an oath to defend them, because I come from a place where they do not exist. I can perhaps see more clearly the blessings of America because they were once new to me. And because I hold those freedoms so dear, I often find myself explaining them to others, to make my passion for America theirs, as well.

There is a joke I've told a time or two at dinner parties with Muslim friends, immigrants like us but more recent ones. It involves a rookie American diplomat, a very green assistant posted to a developing country, perhaps one that has been controlled by autocrats and mullahs for a generation or two. A country like, say, Pakistan. On his very first day, there is a ferocious protest in the street in front of the embassy, hundreds of people chanting "Death to America," burning American flags, proclaiming the United States to be the Great Satan and the enemy of Islam. It goes on for hours, and the crowd is working itself into a dangerous froth. All of the senior diplomats are growing worried, afraid the building might be overrun.

"I got this," the rookie says.

All of the experienced people give him confused looks. They whisper among themselves. He hasn't even been here for a full day. What can he possibly do?

The new guy goes to the main door with a bullhorn. "Gentlemen," he says, because the protesters would almost all be men, "we hear your complaints, and we respect your right to protest."

The crowd quiets, but only to hear what he is saying.

"Now," he goes on, "all of you who would like to continue protesting, remain here. And anyone who would like to apply for a visa to the United States, go to the door at the far left of the building. We'll have the paperwork waiting."

The protest ends immediately as almost the entire crowd stampedes to get their visa applications.

Perhaps it is not laugh-out-loud funny. The point is that such protests are often theater, a ritual venting of misplaced anger. Given the choice, most people in developing countries would flock to America. It is revered as a place of opportunity, a nation built — and still being built — by immigrants, a land where the rule of law prevails, where the cops don't need to be bribed, where one can work hard to provide for his family and create a life that in other parts of the world is only a bitter fantasy.

And yet it is possible, and common, for people to hold two opposing thoughts in their head. One, America is the Promised Land, because it retains that mythic stature. Two, America is anti-Islam, because there has been, in some countries, decades of indoctrination to that notion. A person can, strange as it seems, love America and simultaneously believe America does not love Muslims, that it is foundationally anti-Islamic.

I've told that joke in a number of circumstances and to different audiences, but the reason I would tell it to immigrant friends invariably was because the conversation had turned to the supposed anti-Islamic nature of America. When I was finished and everyone was nodding with rueful recognition, I would pull out my Constitution and lay it on the table. "Show me," I would say. "Show me where in the Constitution America is against Islam. Show me what is incompatible with the teachings of my faith."

I would say this calmly, of course. I was never belligerent, and I was always careful not to ruin an otherwise perfectly pleasant evening. And no one could ever point to a clause or a passage that is objectively offensive to Muslims or antithetical to the teachings of Islam, because there are none. The Declaration and the Constitution are no more anti-Islamic than they are anti-Belgian, which is to say not at all. The holy book of Islam and the founding documents of the United States are wholly unrelated, one theological and one secular. The only connection is that the First Amendment ensures there will be no infringement on the practice of Islam, or of any other religion.

The separation of civil governance and religious faith has always been a fundamental righteousness of the American system. In my own small way, I had quietly devoted myself to preserving that separation — not from any imposition of U.S. law on Islam, but from attempts to subvert the law with religious quackery.

In 1999, for example, a real estate developer in Arizona, a man with millions of dollars and several girlfriends, wanted to divorce his wife. They had married twenty years earlier in Egypt, where they'd both been born and where they'd entered into a marriage contract similar to the one Ghazala and I had signed. According to it, the terms of their separation were that she would receive a house in which to continue raising their children and nothing more, no part of the millions amassed during the course of their marriage. The husband's attorneys browbeat her with that contract, insisting it was the equivalent of a prenuptial agreement. At a hearing, they even called a local imam to testify to its legitimacy. "Aren't you a Muslim?" they asked her, almost accusingly. "Do you reject Islamic law?"

Yes, she was, and, no, she did not. But Islamic law — which as a practical matter is a hodgepodge of religious doctrine tangled over hundreds of years with French and English colonial laws — was irrelevant. As it is typically imposed, it has little to do with equal protection of all parties, but rather protects and rewards the favored few. It generally is repugnantly sexist as well, and what is often called "Islamic law" tends to get its authority less from the actual teachings of the Prophet, peace be upon him, than from men who anoint themselves his interpreters.

The wife needed someone to explain this in court, which is how I got involved. Attorneys who'd studied the law in Muslim countries and at Harvard are a rare breed, but the wife happened to know someone who knew me and asked for my help.

I flew to Phoenix, met her at her lawyer's office. She was a confident, assertive lady, yet bewildered by this turn of events. "Look," I told her, "I'm going to appear and explain why this is hogwash."

On the stand, the husband's attorneys objected to my appearing as an expert on Islamic law. "Your Honor," I said, "I'm just here to see that the injustice is not continued. I'm an expert only on where this unfairness begins."

The judge allowed me to testify. I explained that the parties to a marriage contract had to be equals — "A slave and slaveholder," I said, "cannot sign a valid contract." My point was that the husband was relying on a decades-old religious formality from a foreign country to interpret American law. Why wouldn't Arizona family law apply? Was that reserved for Christians? Was equal protection of the laws denied to immigrants of a different faith? Could an imam really persuade His Honor to ignore the Fourteenth Amendment to the Constitution?

The judge called a recess. The husband's attorneys conferred. They offered her $2 million to settle. "Stand firm," I counseled. "Allow the judge to apply the law, especially now that he knows they tried to hoodwink him."

She did. And she got half of everything.

I testified or advised in a few other cases over the years, always on behalf of women being bullied with fraudulent claims disguised as religion, which is, I suppose, a pet peeve of mine, a recurring irritant. The occasional claims that some Muslims want "sharia law" to be imposed on the United States are in part fueled by hired guns making preposterous claims on behalf of men, ones who've benefited in other countries from generations of theocratic sexism. As both a Muslim and an American, I am twice offended by such malignant foolishness.

Eleven years, five months, and twenty-nine days after Captain Humayun Khan was killed serving his country, Donald Trump was on my television screen. I was familiar with him in the same way most Americans were, as a reality television personality turned improbable candidate for the Republican presidential nomination. He was standing behind a lectern, wearing a dark suit and red tie, and the way the camera framed him, only part of his ubiquitous slogan was visible — MERICA GREAT, in white against a blue background. He was speaking to a crowd of raucous supporters.

"Should I read you the statement?" he asked. He was referring to a press release his campaign had put out earlier that day, December 7, 2015. The crowd clapped and cheered and whistled.

Trump stared at a sheet of paper in his hands. "Donald J. Trump," he began, "is calling for a total and complete shutdown of Muslims" — he lifted his right hand, flicked it as he exaggerated the first syllable, *Moos*-lims — "entering the United States until our country's representatives can figure out" — he looked up, widened his eyes, and went off script, adding words, and in a thumping cadence for effect — "what the hell is going on!"

More cheering and whistling and clapping.

"We have no choice," Trump said, as if that statement was no more or less apparent than the color of the sky. "We. Have. No. Choice."

Five days earlier, on December 2, a husband and wife in San Bernardino, California, had attacked a gathering of public health department workers at a training session and Christmas party. They shot to death fourteen people and wounded more than twenty others. It was a terrible, vicious attack, one condemned and mourned by all people of goodwill. It was also one of three hundred and seventy-two mass shootings in the United States that year, in which four hundred and seventy-five people were killed and almost nineteen hundred were injured. But the San Bernardino shooters happened to be Muslims; the fact that the husband was a citizen who'd been born in the United States and his wife was a legal permanent resident were, for Trump's purposes, apparently immaterial.

Trump returned to reading from his statement, referring to himself in the third person. "Mr. Trump stated, without looking at the various polling data, 'It's obvious to anybody the hatred is beyond comprehension,' " he said. " 'Where the hatred comes from, and why, we'll have to determine.' " He looked up, seemed to be riffing off his own campaign press. "We're gonna have to figure it out. We have to figure it out. We can't live like this." A brief, dramatic pause. "It's gonna get worse and worse. You're gonna have more World Trade Centers. It's gonna get worse and worse, folks. We could be politically correct and we could be stupid, but it's gonna get worse and worse."

I was disgusted but, I confess, not particularly alarmed. I saw Trump then, as did most people, as an anomaly, an accident of politics, a game show host who would be a political footnote. The presidential primaries hadn't even begun. Surely he would be driven out of the campaign.

"Folks," he said, his voice dropping to a somber whisper, "those days are over. Those days are over. We have to be tough, we have to be smart, we have to be vigilant." Enthusiastic hooting rose up from the audience. "Yes, we have to look at mosques, and we have to respect mosques, but, yes, we have to look at mosques, we have no choice. We have to see what's happening. Because something is happening in there — man, there's anger. There's anger. And we have to know about it. We can't be these people that are sitting back like, like . . . in the World Trade Center, like so many different things. We can't be people that knew what was going on two weeks ago in California, probably for months they knew what was going on and they didn't want to tell anybody. We can't be that. We have to be strong. When we see violations, you have to report those violations, and quickly."

I might have smiled grimly at that last line. I'd had a conversation not much earlier with Shaharyar about that very idea. Of course patriotic Americans need to inform the authorities if they learn of dangerous information. If I overheard two men in a mosque planning to car-bomb Times Square, I would alert the police, just as I would if I heard two men at the car wash or at Costco. The offensive part was the assumption — direct and unsubtle — that somehow this was a special obligation of people who pray in mosques, as if Muslims, by the simple fact of being Muslims, presented a special threat. How many lives would be different, how many people would still be alive, if someone had mentioned the unusual inclinations and activities of Eric Rudolph or Timothy McVeigh?

I didn't watch much more that evening. At the time, Trump's speech, like all of Trump's speeches, seemed little more than an exercise in narcissism. He was playing to the mob, rousing the rabble, appealing to and inflaming the worst devils of our nature. It was grotesque vaudeville, nothing more. And in the end, I presumed, it would not matter. He would not be elected, and even if he was, the things he was suggesting were so patently illegal, so squarely in opposition to the ideals enshrined in the founding documents, that they would never come to pass.

On this topic, I did not need to check my little blue booklet for confirmation. There was no need to fish it from my coat hanging in the foyer, where it rested, as always, in the left breast pocket. Perhaps, in hindsight, that was divine guidance. Maybe the things we hold most dear, we keep closest to our hearts.

My cellphone rang early the next afternoon, just after lunch. I didn't recognize the number, but that wasn't unusual. Unfamiliar numbers were not unheard-of, and I had no reason to suspect I'd be receiving harassing phone calls. I assumed whoever was calling was related to my work.

"Mr. Khan?" the voice on the other end of the call said when I answered. "My name is James King and I'm a reporter for a website called *Vocativ.*"

I had never heard of *Vocativ* or of James King, but he was pleasant and respectful. "Yes," I said. "What can I do for you?"

"Well, I'm sorry to bother you, but I was

hoping I might be able to talk to you for a few minutes about Donald Trump wanting to ban Muslims from entering the country. I know your son was killed serving in Iraq, and I thought you might want to say something in response."

It had not occurred to me to say (or not say) anything to a reporter, I suppose because none had ever asked me to respond to a presidential candidate before. I had nothing prepared, no profound insights or practiced, pithy quips. If I considered anything before I answered him, it was this: Why shouldn't I respond, as a Muslim and a patriot? I had opinions based on experience, both joyous and tragic. The words, somewhat to my surprise, came easily.

"Yes, thank you," I said. "I believe I would like to respond. That I should respond. And the first thing I would say is that Donald Trump's ban will never happen."

"Why do you say that?"

"Because Americans are decent and patriotic. I'm very concerned about the level of discourse in politics, but Donald Trump is too divisive for Americans to accept even as a candidate, let alone as president. So that's why I say that it will never happen. Also, it's unconstitutional. We have freedom of religion in the United States. One man can't keep people out because of their religion."

Ghazala was watching me. I mouthed that I was talking to a reporter, and she listened to my side of the conversation, nodding thoughtfully in agreement.

"Muslims are Americans, Muslims are citizens," I said. "Muslims participate in the well-being of this country as American citizens. We are proud American citizens. It's the values that brought us here, not our religion. Trump's position on these issues does not reflect those values."

King asked about the murders in San Bernardino earlier that month, the same ones Trump had cited, and I recounted the conversation I'd had with my son. "This is the time for us American Muslims to rat out any traitor who walks among us," I told King. "This is high time for Muslims to stand firm. Among us hide the enemies of the value system of this country. And we need to defend it. And if it means ratting out the traitors who hide behind an American passport, that's what we need to do."

We shifted away from that topic, a tangent, really, as I do not believe Muslims, as a group, are any more or less patriotic than any other demographic. I told King how Ghazala and I used to take the boys to the Jefferson Memorial, how we would read each of the inscriptions carved inside, how we instilled those ideals in our children. And that brought us to Captain Humayun Khan.

"We still wonder what made him take those ten steps," I said, explaining how he'd walked toward the taxi. "Maybe that's the point where all the values, all the service to the country, all the things he learned in this country kicked in."

I watched Ghazala. Her eyes were wet with tears.

"It was those values that made him take those ten steps. Those ten steps told us we did not make a mistake in moving to this country. These were the values we wanted to adopt. Not religious values — human values."

We spoke for twenty minutes or so, eventually returning to the bitterness of politics, even then, before the primaries had properly begun. "This country is not strong because of its economic power or military power," I said. "This country is strong because of its values, and during this political season, we all need to keep that in mind."

King thanked me for my time, offered his condolences, and we ended the call, which had been quite pleasant, considering the subject. He wrote a short story, nine paragraphs, that was posted on the *Vocativ* website later that day. THE FATHER OF A MUSLIM WAR HERO HAS THIS TO SAY TO DONALD TRUMP, the headline read. It was an accurate recounting of our conversation, neither shrill nor framed as an attack — just a reasoned response from one man who was taking a well-informed position on a policy Trump was proposing, about which, since I'd been asked, I did indeed have something to say.

I was not a political activist. I did not make a habit of speaking publicly about candidates or causes. My commentary had never before been sought on matters of national, or even local, import. If anyone else called, I supposed I would answer. But I also assumed no one else would call.

Hillary Clinton's campaign called the next day. A woman from the communications staff said she'd read the *Vocativ* story.

"Secretary Clinton would like to do a tribute to Captain Khan next week in Minnesota," she told me. "That is, if you're comfortable with it. We can prepare something and show it to you."

I paused. This, obviously, was a significantly different scenario. It is one thing to speak with a reporter, quite another for my son to be focused on, even briefly, by the woman widely expected to be the next president of the United States. That is not so much a spotlight as a floodlight. Then again, I wasn't being asked to offer anything other than my permission, which, as a practical matter, the Clinton campaign didn't require. Their request was a respectful courtesy.

"I think that would be fine," I said, after I'd quickly processed my thoughts. "I would like to see it, yes, if that would be okay."

Six days later, on December 15, 2015, Clinton gave a speech at the University of Minnesota about homeland security or, more precisely, about defeating people who commit acts of terrorism in the name of what they say is Islam. She made only quick mentions of the first two parts of a three-part plan, namely defeating ISIS in the Middle East and defeating radical jihadists around the world. "I want to focus today on the third part of my plan," she said. "How we defend our country and prevent radicalization here at home."

She talked about preventing recruitment of alienated young people, about preventing terrorists from getting weapons, about disrupting attacks before they can be staged, about supporting law enforcement. She criticized Republicans and Democrats alike.

But when she spoke of my son, of Humayun, it was outside the context of politics or policy.

She quoted our first president — "As George Washington put it, the United States gives 'to bigotry no sanction, to persecution no assistance' " — and our forty-third, George W. Bush, who, after 9/11, "declared that those who attempt to intimidate or discriminate against our Muslim citizens 'don't represent the best of America . . . they represent the worst of humankind.' "

Then she said, "If you want to see the best of America, you need look no further than Army Captain Humayun Khan."

She went on to tell the story of Humayun's death. She quoted what I'd told James King, about the ten steps and how we knew we hadn't made a mistake moving here.

"As hard as this is," she said, "it's time to move from fear to resolve. It's time to stand up and say, 'We are Americans.' "

Ghazala and I did not see such patriotic words as politicizing Humayun's death. Granted, they were offered in part as a rebuke to Donald Trump, but only the same one I'd given a few days earlier. Those few lines, quoting Washington and Bush and insisting we are all Americans, were neither

Democratic nor Republican. No patriot could reasonably argue with them, nor even attempt to.

A video of that portion of her speech, just two minutes and ten seconds, was put online. Except for the logo in the lower right corner, there was no hint of partisan politics. We did not feel as if we'd been co-opted into a campaign. If it was difficult to watch, that was only because Clinton was recounting the death of our son. No matter how poetic the prose, how heartfelt the tribute, those are words no parent ever wants to hear.

Winter melted into spring. The political season came into full, ferocious bloom, but for us it was only background color. Omer's first son, our fourth grandchild, was born, a moment of joy and celebration.

A few days after his arrival, I wandered into the kitchen. The stove was full with simmering pots, and the countertops were cluttered with bowls and pans and ingredients parceled out for dozens of dishes. Ghazala was humming, flitting from one station to the next, stirring and chopping and mixing.

"What's all this?" I asked.

"It's for the party," she said, not breaking

her rhythm.

"All *this*. All this food?"

"Well, yes, we have a lot of guests." Ghazala freed a hand long enough to slide a sheet of paper toward me.

I looked at it incredulously. There must have been three dozen names on it.

"No," I said. "No, this won't do. This is too much. We barely know some of these people."

"Our grandson is born only once," Ghazala said, not looking up from her cooking. "It's a celebration."

"But this is absolutely extravagant," I said. I've never been one for extravagance, but I was surprised by the sharpness of my tone. "I know you want to show your happiness, but this is too much. This is showing off."

I paused, waiting for an answer. Ghazala continued her work, ignoring my mood, happy in her preparations for the party.

I stalked out of the room.

My mother had died nine years earlier, from a massive heart attack after living for years with diabetes and generally declining health. Had she been with us, though, she would have found me in the living room and sat quietly next to me. "Now, Muazzam," she would have said, as she'd said so many times, "listen to Ghazala. You know she is right." And I would have continued to sulk stubbornly — I'm not prone to confrontation — even as I knew that my mother was correct.

She and Ghazala were so similar in their demeanor, in their eternal patience, in their belief that every moment, no matter how tense, will pass. I believe that is partly why they were so close. In family matters, I was always better off deferring to Ghazala. When the boys were in high school, for instance, they sometimes chose elective courses that I thought were foolish, and I would lecture them about why they should pick more rigorous subjects. They would hear me out, and then go gripe to Ghazala, who would come to me later. "Lecturing them is not the right way to guide them to the proper choices," she would tell me. When I would start to protest, my mother would always be there, calmly whispering, "Listen to Ghazala."

I should not have been surprised at Ghazala's exuberance over our grandson. She has always honored family above all else — both the elders who preceded us and the grandchildren who came next. On the anniversary of our parents' deaths, she always gathers the family for a special dinner to honor them. Every May 30, she cooks Afghani pilau and shami kebabs, her father's favorite dishes; there is eggplant for her mother and rice pudding for my father. Each June 20, the anniversary of my mother's passing, she prepares a feast of either goat or chicken stewed with potatoes and gravy, fried rice, and a sweet yellow rice. Ghazala nurtures a connection between our grandchildren and the great-grandparents they have never known, reminding us all that we are part of something larger.

None of this understanding precluded me from going to bed in a foul mood that night. But by morning, I'd softened. I was over-joyed, too, and I supposed I could tolerate one excessively festive day. I went down to the kitchen, where Ghazala was busily cook-ing again.

She poured me a cup of coffee. "Would you like me to warm you a croissant?" she asked.

Her tone was breezy, carefree. She did not ask me about my mood or if I'd changed my mind or if I was ready to apologize for being so petulant. She did not mention my outburst at all, but rather had chosen to forgive me my minor trespass.

"Yes, please," I said. "That would be nice."

We had been married for forty-one years. There had been bumps along the way, minor ones, nothing even worth writing about. They had remained mere bumps because of Ghazala's immense capacity to forgive, quickly and fully. In any relationship worth preserving, there will be difficulties, moments of tribulation. But they will pass, and become only vaguely recalled inconveniences, if one chooses to look beyond them, to remember the strength of the foundation and not obsess about a temporary crack in the façade.

The spring started to warm. Even as Donald Trump whittled away his Republican opponents, I held fast to my belief in the decency of the American people. His ability to capture a plurality of the fractured Republican primary base was disconcerting, but those voters were a fraction of a fraction of a fraction of the country.

When he secured the nomination, in late May 2016, I was badly disappointed. Had it really been only twenty-seven years since Ronald Reagan spoke so movingly of the shining city? Trump's city was a frightened, isolated fortress, walled off from Mexicans and Muslims, from all the *others*. His America was crumbling and weak, a dreary landscape implicit in his slogan: To make America great again, one had to assume that it was not in fact great now.

Most Americans surely do not share that vision, so I was certain that a majority of November's voters would reject his increasingly divisive rhetoric, his childish taunts, his thuggish calls to beat up protesters, his blatant disregard for, and disrespect of, our fundamental values. To me, Trump was a distressing anomaly, but only temporary, a flash of passing madness, a fluke who would be soundly rejected in the end.

In early July, another person from the Clinton campaign called to invite Ghazala and me to the Democratic National Convention in Philadelphia. Several Gold Star families, we were told, would be attending, and the clip of Clinton paying tribute to Humayun would be projected on the giant screens in the convention center. We accepted. We were aware that airing the piece on the final night of the convention, when Clinton would speak and the largest audience would be watching, risked turning our son into political fodder, but we were not necessarily uncomfortable with that. Humayun died an apolitical death. Nothing Clinton had said, and nothing we had done, had changed that. If having one candidate call him "the best of America" was now to be considered crass, then we had already careened down a dark and dangerous road.

A few days later, though, that same campaign aide called again.

"We were thinking," he said, "that you might want to speak."

I paused, instinctively cautious. "What do you mean?" I said after a moment.

"I mean, you and Mrs. Khan would go on stage right after the tribute and say a few words," he said. "It wouldn't be long. The schedule is very tight. Two minutes, tops."

I was quiet again for a moment. "Can we think about it?"

"Yes, of course. Take a few days and think about it. But let us know as soon as you can. We think it would be very powerful."

"Don't do it, Baba."

My sons shook their heads slowly, emphatically.

"Why not?" I asked. "What would be wrong with speaking?"

They sighed heavily. "I just don't see any good coming of it," one said. "You've seen how ugly politics has gotten. Do you really want to get in the middle of that? Do you really want to put *us* in the middle of that?"

I nodded because I understood, and I couldn't disagree. For two days, Ghazala and I had asked friends, our children, other

355

relatives, if we should take the proffered podium. They were unanimous in saying no.

I could mount an argument for why I should speak. Over the years, I had come to see the world as divided roughly into two groups: those who have freedom, and those who want it. Take the Bill of Rights to the farthest edge of the world, to the remotest village where no one has heard of the United States, and read it. Ask people if they want to have the right to speak freely, to worship freely, and they will say yes. Ask them if they want to be free from the police rousting them from their homes for no good reason, and they will say yes. Ask them if they want to be able to protect themselves, and ask them if they think the law should treat everyone the same, and they will say yes. Those are the First, Fourth, Second, and Fourteenth Amendments. You could go through the entire Constitution, distill it into common language, and people will want those things. They will want them because they are universal dignities, human dignities.

The American experiment is the ideal to which all people aspire. Perhaps not in the particulars of policy or politics, but in the foundation, in the elegance of the original ideals. Yet one political party had nominated as its candidate a man who openly threatened those freedoms, who gleefully assaulted the basic concept of human dignity. For months, neighbors had been telling us about children of Latino and Indian families being mocked and bullied at school, told that Trump would kick them out of the country. His rallies thrummed with all the subtlety of a beer hall putsch. He encouraged his followers to physically abuse protesters. He literally put reporters in a pen and called them out, often by name, as liars and scum. He was loosing a wildness upon the land, stirring the worst of human nature.

Even if I had only two minutes, perhaps I could find words to remind us all what liberty truly is, why it matters, and why we must defend it for all people. I wasn't a celebrity and I wasn't an orator, only a humble man who loved his country. Wasn't I almost required, by conscience and patriotism, to speak up?

At the same time, I suspected everyone was correct to wonder: at what cost, and for what benefit? Clinton, everyone still believed, would win in November; whatever I said would have little, if any, impact on the election's outcome. But in the months until then, might we become additional targets for Trump? Being Gold Star parents was no insulation. He had mocked a disabled reporter. He had mocked Senator McCain, one of my son's heroes, for suffering through years in a prisoner-of-war camp, years Trump spent avoiding the war altogether. Ted Cruz was Lyin' Ted and Marco Rubio was Little Marco and Clinton was Crooked Hillary. Would his more fanatical followers harass my sons, my grandchildren, Ghazala and me?

After discussing it with everyone else, Ghazala and I sat down one morning, went through the pros and cons again, and decided we would decline. It wasn't worth it.

"I'll call them later this afternoon and let them know," I said.

I puttered around until lunch. In the early afternoon, I walked down the driveway to the edge of the road, where our mailbox is perched on a post stuck in the grass. I opened it, expecting to collect a stack of bills and flyers and solicitations, but it was empty except for a single small envelope. It was addressed simply to "Mr. Khan." There was no stamp and no return address.

The top flap released easily when I slid my finger under it. I pulled out a plain card, pale yellow. Inside, I recognized a child's handwriting. "Dear Mr. Khan," it said. "You are a lawyer. Can you please not let them deport Maria? She is in fifth grade and she is our friend. Thank you."

I stood by the mailbox, reading the note a few times or maybe just staring at it. I walked back up the driveway, climbed the steps through the azalea bushes, and went inside to the room with the bay windows.

Humayun stared from the wall. Such kind eyes.

I asked myself, *What would Humayun do?*

My grandfather, in my memory, sits on the edge of my bed. The evening is beginning to cool, but the moon has not yet crossed over the courtyard.

"Many years ago," he tells me, "a famous grammarian came to a river that he needed to get across. You know what a grammarian is, yes?"

I shook my head.

"He's someone who studies grammar, knows everything there is to know about grammar, where to put the commas and the periods and all the rules. And he had to get across this river. Fortunately, there was a boatman nearby — I know you know what a boatman is — and he agreed to take the grammarian. The grammarian gets in the boat and, with an air of great superiority, he tells the boatman what he does. 'Have you learned any grammar?' he asks the boatman.

" 'No,' the boatman says. 'I've been learning to row this boat and navigate this river ever since I was a small child, and I missed all of my schooling.'

"The grammarian lets out a big sigh. 'You've wasted half your life,' he says, 'by not learning any grammar.' The boatman doesn't seem at all bothered by this. He just keeps rowing. But when they get to the middle of the river, the water begins to swirl, faster and faster, until it becomes a whirlpool. 'Row this boat out of this whirlpool, my handsome man,' the grammarian says. He's starting to panic.

"But the boatman is very calm. 'Haven't you learned how to swim?' he asks. And the grammarian says, 'No, I've never had time. I was studying!' The boatman says to him, 'Then *all* of your life is wasted, because you are going to drown in this whirlpool.' "

That was from Rumi. I'd thought of it often over the years, just as I'd often remembered my father telling me that lading a donkey with books didn't make it a scholar, and Iqbal teaching me to think with both my head and my heart. Pursuits of the mind are important, but what good are they if one doesn't have the practical skills to survive a wild river?

I had all my degrees. I had my notes written in the soft, worn margins of my pocket Constitution. I could quote Jefferson and Washington, and even Scalia. I could speak, thoughtfully and authoritatively, about the wonder of America. I wasn't in danger of drowning in a river, exactly, so it's not a perfect analogy. But if I wouldn't use my accumulated learning for a practical good, what was the point? Those diplomas would be no more than decorations, my knowledge mere trivia.

Ghazala and I both knew what Humayun would have done in our position. The day I found the note in my mailbox, a child asking for help in a more hateful America, I called the Clinton campaign and accepted their invitation.

I practiced what I would say in front of Ghazala. "And unlike Donald Trump's wife," I read aloud, "I didn't plagiarize my speech."

Ghazala gave me a pained smile. "No, no," she said. "Take that out. Don't go down to their level. We are paying tribute to our son."

I scratched out the line with a pen. Ghazala was an excellent editor. I had looked up how many words were in a two-minute speech, and found it was startlingly few: about two hundred and fifty, though I could push it by a dozen or so. We cut hundreds in the beginning. Losing the bad jokes and the gibes was easy enough; poking Melania Trump for reading, at the Republican convention, parts of a speech originally given years earlier by Michelle Obama would have been unkind, unnecessary, and beside the point. But now we were down to the nip-and-tuck, shaving adjectives and articles. I read draft after draft while Ghazala timed me. "Too long," she said half a dozen times.

Then I climbed the stairs to my office, sat down at the computer, hunted for a few stray words to excise, printed out a new version, and tried again. On the seventh attempt, Ghazala clocked it at just over two minutes:

First, our thoughts and prayers are with our veterans and those who serve today. Tonight, we are honored to stand here as the parents of Captain Humayun Khan, and as patriotic American Muslims with undivided loyalty to our country.

Like many immigrants, we came to this country empty-handed. We believed in American democracy — that with hard work and the goodness of this country, we could share in and contribute to its blessings.

We were blessed to raise our three sons in a nation where they were free to be themselves and follow their dreams. Our son, Humayun, had dreams of being a military lawyer. But he put those dreams aside the day he sacrificed his life to save his fellow soldiers.

Hillary Clinton was right when she called my son "the best of America." If it was up to Donald Trump, he never would have been in America. Donald Trump consistently smears the character of Muslims. He disrespects other minorities — women, judges, even his own party leadership. He vows to build walls and ban us from this country.

Donald Trump, you are asking Americans to trust you with our future. Let me ask you: Have you even read the United States Constitution? I will gladly lend you my copy. In this document, look for the words "liberty" and "equal protection of law."

Have you ever been to Arlington Cemetery? Go look at the graves of the brave patriots who died defending America —

you will see all faiths, genders, and eth-nicities.

You have sacrificed nothing and no one.

We can't solve our problems by building walls and sowing division. We are stronger together. And we will keep getting stronger when Hillary Clinton becomes our next president.

It was a good speech, we thought. Tight, almost blunt, heartfelt, angry without raging. We'd gotten in *liberty* and *equal protection of law* (which, not incidentally, is one word shorter than "equal protection of *the* law"). We criticized Trump by simply restating his own positions and, near the end, the plain fact that he has had to make no sacrifices for all of the blessings and riches America has provided him and his family.

But most important, we were honoring Humayun. Explicitly, yes, but also implicitly. Every word was infused with his spirit, his soul. Captain Humayun Khan knew that problems cannot be solved by building walls and sowing division. That was how he lived. He will always be with us, and we were grateful for the chance to share him with the world.

In the backseat of a taxi in Philadelphia, I

patted my pockets again, checking for coins or keys, anything metal. It was early on the evening on July 28, the fourth and last night of the Democratic convention. The theme for the evening was "Stronger Together," which was also Clinton's campaign slogan, and we were scheduled to speak near the end of the lineup, only a few slots before Clinton herself. Or, rather, I would be speaking. We knew the evening would be excruciatingly difficult for Ghazala, that just standing on the stage without dissolving into tears would be an act of exceptional strength. I'd asked her to say just a few words, a quick thank-you for honoring Humayun. She said she couldn't bear even that. "You know as soon as I open my mouth," she told me, "I'm going to collapse." So she would stand by my side, and I would speak for both of us.

We'd been warned by the convention staff to remove any metal before we arrived. Security was tight, and pinging the metal detectors would slow us down. I'd carefully searched my pockets before we left the Holiday Inn, emptied them of anything that might set off an alarm. But I checked again in the cab. Nerves.

I brushed my hands down the thighs of my trousers, felt only smooth fabric where the pockets were. I reached into my suit coat, my left hand poking into the right pocket, then switching, my right hand into the left.

My fingertips bumped against a thin row of ridges. My Constitution.

I'd forgotten it was there.

"Look at this," I said to Ghazala, shimmering like a sapphire in a blue hijab next to me. I pulled the booklet out and held it up with a quick, authoritative snap, like a magician showing her the queen of diamonds.

She raised her eyebrows.

"What do you think?" I asked. "Should I pull it out? When I say, 'I will gladly lend you my copy,' should I hold it up?" I repeated the motion, maybe with a little more drama.

Ghazala smiled. "Yes, I think that would be very powerful," she said. "But you should ask for permission from the campaign organizers before you do that. And don't do it like that."

"Like what?"

"Look," she said. "You're showing me the back. All they'll see is a blank blue page. Turn it over."

I turned it over so the cover faced her.

"Now put it back in your pocket and take

it out again."

I followed her instructions, making sure I held it the same way going in and coming out.

"Yes, perfect," she said. "Just like that. Make sure you have it the right way in your pocket."

We practiced a few more times in the backseat of the taxi, figuring out the most effective timing. *I will gladly lend you my copy* — pull it out. Or pull it out, then *I will gladly lend you my copy.* No, in the middle, *I will glad* — pull it out —*ly lend you my copy.* Then a more vigorous shake, almost a waggle, to make the snap more obvious.

Yes, we agreed, that would work well.

In the green room inside the convention hall, we found the campaign staffer who'd invited us. I showed him my little blue booklet. "I was thinking," I told him, "that I could pull this out when I offer to lend Donald Trump my copy. What do you think?"

His eyes widened. "Really? Are you comfortable with that?"

"Yes, of course."

He put his hands on my shoulders, took a step in closer. "That," he said, "would be incredible. That would be *a moment.*"

The early-evening lineup was just getting

started, so we waited in the green room with the later speakers. We met General John Allen, a retired four-star general from the Marine Corps who would go on after us. He was very warm. "I want you to know how grateful we are for Captain Khan's service," he said. "And for his family's, for your service in continuing to care for this nation." There was also a very tall, light-skinned black man there. He was familiar, but I couldn't place him until he approached me.

He held out a massive hand. "Mr. Khan," he said. "I'm Kareem Abdul-Jabbar. It's such an honor to meet you. I'm going to be introducing you tonight."

My throat tightened, and I could feel tears welling in my eyes. Was this a sign? Was Humayun there with us?

I swallowed hard, then took his giant hand in both of mine. "Mr. Abdul-Jabbar, I am so humbled," I told him. "You would not know this" — I swallowed again, collected myself — "but you were my son's favorite basketball player."

He looked at me with such gentleness, such compassion. "No," he said, "I wouldn't have known that. And that's very kind of you to tell me. That makes this even more of an honor."

"Yes, thank you," I said. My throat was loosening. "Maybe this is part of the plan. Maybe the Creator is here with us."

Soon, Abdul-Jabbar walked onto the stage. "I'm here to tell you about Captain Humayun Khan," he said, "who was one of fourteen American Muslim soldiers who have died in combat serving the United States since 9/11." He gave a short synopsis of our life in America, told how we visited the Jefferson Memorial almost like a pilgrimage. "The words engraved there read, 'I have sworn upon the altar of God eternal hostility against every form of tyranny over the mind of man,'" he said. "Donald Trump's idea to register Muslims and prevent them from entering our country is the very tyranny Jefferson abhorred."

He continued the contrast, comparing Jefferson's Virginia Statute for Religious Freedom, which was the model for the First Amendment, to modern "religious freedom" laws, like one signed by Mike Pence when he was governor of Indiana, which are nothing of the sort but rather codified oppression. Then he ended with a rallying call to reject the fear that breeds discrimination. "Those who think Americans scare easily enough to abandon our country's ideals in exchange for a false sense of security underestimate our resolve," he said. "To them, we say only this: Not here, not ever."

Abdul-Jabbar left the stage to thunderous applause.

The video screens switched to Clinton. The two minutes from her speech in Minnesota began to play. The hall fell silent. The video clip finished.

Humayun's portrait went up on the screens.

Then it was our turn. We were waiting just offstage, Ghazala close to my right side, holding my arm. We knew there was a crowd seated out beyond the stage, and millions more people watching us on their televisions. But all we could see were the lights, brilliant and blinding white.

A stage manager signaled it was time.

We stepped forward.

AFTERWORD

Charlottesville, July 2017

Adjacent to the room where we've hung Humayun's portrait and awards and mementos is our dining room, but we rarely eat there anymore. The table, a long slab of polished wood, is covered with cards and letters, hundreds of them, that we've received since the summer of 2016. Some of them have been left on Humayun's grave and some are notes I've been handed while traveling, but most arrive in the mail, often addressed only to "Mr. and Mrs. Khan, Charlottesville, VA." The men and women in the local post office know where they're supposed to go, and they kindly route them to our home.

Someday, Ghazala and I will sort them and box them and store them away. Someday. For now, though, we leave them on the table. Every now and then, I'll pull out one of the chairs and sift through the piles. The

371

return addresses tell us that they are from all over the country, and that some are even from out of the country. Over the course of the year since our speech, I've taken to sitting there often, light filtering through Ghazala's curtains on the big bay windows behind me, and reading through a few of them. I find them both soothing and inspiring, each a reminder of the fundamental decency of people. The words, written by strangers, are invariably kind.

On the top of one pile as I write this is a single sheet, creased from the way it was tightly folded when a flight attendant slipped it to me on my way home from California. It was from a passenger a few rows back on an airplane who must have recognized me when boarding. "I apologize for the wrinkled paper — it's all I've got at the moment and I didn't want to pass on the opportunity to convey my deepest appreciation of and respect for you and your family," it begins. The note continues for a few more lines, then closes with this: "You make me proud to be a citizen in this country." It is signed, "Your fellow American."

My heart swells.

There is another note, neatly typed, on the top of the next stack. It is from a woman in Bend, Oregon, who sent it to us — "Mr. and Mrs. Khan, Charlottesville, VA" — a week after the Democratic convention. I smooth it out, start to read.

She offers her condolences, and writes that she believes Humayun must be proud of us for speaking out. We like to believe so, too. She thanks us for our courage, and for exercising the rights guaranteed to all Americans in the First Amendment to the Constitution. And then this:

> It has been such a sight to behold and you have made me very proud as an American. I am disabled and unable to travel by airplane. I will never be able to see the Statue of Liberty or Ellis Island, but that is OK now because I have seen the parents of Captain Humayun Khan in action and I have seen Lady Liberty quite alive.

I feel the familiar lump in my throat. My emotions are still so easily stirred, imperfectly camouflaged just beneath the dignified calm I try to maintain.

Under that note, I find a scrap of lined paper torn from a pocket-sized notebook: "Dear Mr. and Mrs. Khan," it reads. "I am active duty military and I just wanted to say what an honor it is to meet you. THANK

YOU! Sincerely, An Inspired Citizen."

Ghazala and I never wanted to be political activists. We never wanted to be spokespeople or symbols or characters in an ongoing political drama. This son of Pakistani farmers and great-great-great granddaughter of Afghani royalty wanted only a simple life, to raise our sons to be honorable, respectful, merciful, to offer them a life I could not even have dreamed of when I was a boy. We chose to be patriotic United States citizens, yes, but we did not intend to become public evangelists for American values. We believed that our quiet lives would resume after our brief appearance on stage.

I look down the length of our dining room table, mounds of paper rippling to the far end, small note cards sliding into the valleys between the stacks. It is a sloppy, cluttered mess, yet also evidence of something profound. In our own small way, perhaps we have reminded people of what it means to be an American. Staring at those piles, I am both grateful and deeply humbled.

So when people ask me to speak, I go. The travel can be tiring, but how can I say no? I am a stick that perhaps has become a ney, the grammarian refusing to drown in the whirlpool.

The sun drops low over Constitution

Route, sliding behind the trees that spread a shadow of descending dusk. I sit there in the darkening evening, refolding the letter from Oregon, and then I set it gently with the others.

No river runs alone.

ACKNOWLEDGMENTS

Telling this story, moving it from my memory to the preceding pages, would not have been possible without the assistance of many people.

Jeff Nussbaum and Stephanie Cutter were a source of light when it looked dark outside. Jennifer Joel at ICM has been my true and steady guide from the beginning. Ben Greenberg edited this humble, ordinary story into one infused with patriotism and, I hope, a reflection of what is best about America. London King, Gina Centrello, Susan Kamil, Andy Ward, Avideh Bashirrad, Leigh Marchant, and all my friends at Random House provided invaluable counsel and support. Sean Flynn helped put my thoughts into words. I am grateful for all of them.

The cards and letters sent by strangers and new friends encouraged me to continue speaking about the Constitution and the goodness enshrined within it. To all who wrote, thank you; someday, Ghazala and I will reply to each of you. Thank you, too, to all the people and organizations who've invited us to speak, and to all the people in the media who invited me on their programs and wrote stories about our journey, ignoring my inability at times to speak as coherently as I would prefer. Each of them, individually and institutionally, provides hope in a difficult time for my country. Thousands of people have listened to me speak, have asked questions, have offered a handshake, an embrace, a kind and sympathetic word — in every one of those people, I have seen and felt the presence of my Creator. They are all sacred to me, and I thank them for joining on this voyage.

I offer my gratitude to the University of Virginia, which allowed us to continue our son's legacy through the establishment of the Capt. Humayun S. Khan Memorial Scholarship. It will be funded from the proceeds I received from this book, and will be awarded to a deserving student based on need each year.

Shaharyar and Omer have unfailingly provided love, respect, and wise counsel. I am grateful to them, their spouses, and our grandchildren, who are, of course, our pride and joy.

I remain indebted to my siblings, all nine of them, who gave me more than my share while they ate less and wore less; to my parents and grandparents, who blessed me with their love and guidance, who instilled in me generosity, decency, and an abiding faith in humanity; and to Ghazala's parents, who accepted me when I had done nothing to deserve their daughter.

Without Ghazala, none of this — the book and, more important, the decades that came before — would have been possible. She has always been the center of gravity in our family, the source of the pure goodness I see in our children. She has given me her unconditional love and companionship for forty-four years, despite my failures and flaws. For that, I am more thankful than I can possibly express, and will be forever.

Finally, I am grateful Humayun graced our lives for twenty-seven years. The light of his candle shines even now, a glow that bring us comfort despite the ache of his physical absence. It has been my highest honor to share that light.

ABOUT THE AUTHOR

Khizr Khan, the eldest of ten children, was born in rural Pakistan in 1950. He moved to the United States with his wife, Ghazala, in 1980. The couple became American citizens and raised their three sons in Silver Spring, Maryland. Their middle son, U.S. Army captain Humayun Khan, a graduate of the University of Virginia and its Army ROTC program, was killed in 2004 while stopping a suicide attack near Baqubah, Iraq, and was posthumously awarded a Purple Heart and Bronze Star. Khizr Khan holds a B.A. degree from the University of the Punjab, an LL.B. from Punjab University Law College, and an LL.M. from Harvard Law School. He is a member of the Bar of the Supreme Court of the United States, the District of Columbia Bar, the New York State Bar, and the American Bar Association. Khan's law practice includes complex civil litigation, electronic discovery, health privacy compliance law, and civil rights and veterans' rights advocacy. He and Ghazala live in Charlottesville, Virginia.